SENECA

THE CLIMBER'S GUIDE

**REVISED
EDITION**

**Tony
Barnes**

SENECA:
THE CLIMBER'S GUIDE
Revised Edition

Tony Barnes

COVER DESIGN: John Nedwidek, emdesign

MAPS: Mark Robinson

FRONT COVER: Harrison Schull on SPINNAKER (5.10c) Photo: Darell Hensley
West Face Seneca Rocks Photo: Darell Hensley
North Peak - West Face Photo: Tony Barnes

ISBN: 0-9643698-1-8

ACKNOWLEDGMENTS

In 1975, Rich Pleiss and Bill Webster co-edited a guidebook to climbing at Seneca Rocks that contained descriptions of 121 routes. Webster went on to edit five more editions, finishing his 6th Seneca guidebook in 1990. That book described 377 routes, more than double the number recorded in his previous edition. This book, which describes over 400 routes, owes its existence to his work of fifteen years.

Many other individuals contributed to the body of knowledge that was passed down over the years, including F.R. Robinson, John Christian, Rich Pleiss, and John Stannard. This lineage — and for any omission the editor apologizes —depended on the many climbers whose first ascent and repeat ascent experiences were passed along to them. Thanks are due to all those who care about Seneca, and have contributed to this book.

In particular, and I hope I've remembered everyone, special thanks to: Bill Webster, Don Hubbard, Howard Doyle, Dan Miller, Tom Cecil, John and Helen Markwell, Darell Hensley, Greg Smith, Ed Begoon, Karen Jacobson, Harrison Shull, and Casey Rucker.

IMPORTANT SAFETY INFORMATION
PLEASE READ THE MATERIAL ON THIS PAGE BEFORE USING THE GUIDE!

Rock climbing, ice climbing, bouldering, and mountaineering are sports which may be extremely dangerous and which may lead to severe injury or death. This book is a guide to rock climbing in one particular area within the State of West Virginia. Before using this guide, it is extremely important that the user understand the limitations that may be found in these pages.

1. This is a guidebook to climbing routes. It is not a climbing instruction manual. Climbers should receive adequate instruction before using this guide.

2. This guide consists of information compiled from a number of different sources. Much of the information has not been personally verified by the editor. Topos, lines on photographs, and written descriptions may contain inaccurate information.

3. The user who wishes to climb safely must have a strong working knowledge of, and experience with, current climbing methods, including methods of protecting climbing routes, rope handling, retreat from rocks and mountains, and emergency response.

4. Climbers must rely on their own personal judgment in all climbing situations. This guidebook should be used to supplement the climber's personal knowledge, skill, and judgment. Information found in the guidebook should not be used as a substitute for personal judgment, especially in situations which have the potential for injury or death.

5. Difficulty ratings and descriptions found in this guide are subjective. The ratings are used in an attempt to give climbers a general feel for the relative difficulty of climbing routes. Where possible the editor uses consensus ratings generally in use in the local climbing community. Many routes, particularly those which are not popular, may not have consensus ratings. Individuals may not agree on ratings for a variety of reasons.

6. Protection ratings and descriptions found in this guide are subjective. The ratings are used in an attempt to give climbers a general feel for the relative danger of climbing routes. Where possible the editor uses consensus ratings generally in use in the local climbing community. Many routes, particularly those which are not popular, may not have consensus ratings. Individuals may not agree on ratings for a variety of reasons. All routes have the potential for injury or death regardless of whether or not they have a "R" or "X" protection rating.

7. This book refers to fixed protection such as pitons and bolts. The editor cannot guarantee that these fixed protection points are still in place (they are sometimes removed by human as well as by natural causes). Further, it is important to know that the editor cannot guarantee the integrity of any feature described in this book, including bolts, pitons, rock features, vegetation, or other features.

THE EDITOR AND PUBLISHER OF THIS GUIDE OFFER NO WARRANTY, WHETHER EXPRESSED OR IMPLIED, THAT THE INFORMATION CONTAINED HEREIN IS ACCURATE. THE USE OF THIS BOOK FOR THE PURPOSE OF CLIMBING INDICATES THAT YOU UNDERSTAND ITS LIMITATIONS AND AGREE TO ACCEPT RESPONSIBILITY FOR YOUR OWN ACTIONS IN WHAT IS POTENTIALLY A LIFE THREATENING SPORT.

TABLE OF CONTENTS

When you're going to take risks –
You don't want to take chances.

- Quality Gear
- Shoe & Helmet Rentals
- Magazines & Books
- Maps

- Friendly Front Porch
- Picnic Tables
- Bulletin Board
- Bouldering Wall

EST. 1971

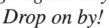

*W*e are the original climbing shop & guide service at Seneca Rocks. Staffed by knowledgeable professionals who live here, the school and shop have been providing the best equipment, training, guided climbs and general information for going on 25 years.
Drop on by!

– *Behind Harper's Country Store* –

1-(800)-548-0108
(304) 567-2600

INTRODUCTION

One goal of this guide is to offer the reader a sense of Seneca's unique culture which is composed of its environment, people, and climbing history. Guidebooks are important repositories of knowledge about the areas they describe and in some cases are shapers of the local culture. Guidebooks not only guide and direct climbers, but also inspire and motivate. This book is intended to inform its users about the climbing at Seneca, and to assist the growing number of new climbers to climb safely and use the area in an environmentally friendly manner.

It is in the interest of everyone concerned with the climbing community's future at Seneca that issues of the environment, safety and access be understood. We urge every climber to thoroughly read the introductory materials, especially the sections that deal with general safety information, the use of fixed anchors, the care required in traveling on Seneca's exposed sub-fifth class terrain, and protection of fragile soils and vegetation.

We also encourage everyone to read the history section of this guide. New climbers should understand that Seneca's climbing community has maintained a deep respect for the landscape and for the people who have pushed free climbing limits ever upward. Unlike some other climbing areas in the United States, you will seldom hear the "current" hot climbers disparage the abilities of climbers from past generations. We think this tolerance is due in large part to the tremendous sense of history that exists at Seneca. Each new generation has been able to push standards upward while maintaining the ability to judge their predecessors' accomplishments based on conditions and standards found at the time.

DANGERS OF CLIMBING

The laws of gravity are very, very strict
You're just bending them for your own benefit
– Billy Bragg

Climbing is a potentially dangerous sport. The climber ties on a thin rope, ascends vertical or overhanging rock, places protection from uncertain stances, and climbs high above the ground on a substance that is much harder than the hardest human bone. The climber must rely on the integrity of the rock, which may be questionable. The climber depends on the protection he places, which he may do poorly. The climber must rely on his body, which may not be equal to the challenge. But, most importantly the climber depends on his mental state. This means the climber must choose routes wisely, select an appropriate rack of protection, control panic in difficult situations, make wise decisions under life and death circumstances, and often make decisions based on limited information.

Climbing is potentially dangerous, on rare occasions even lethal, but ultimately one of the most exciting and invigorating sports practiced by modern man. The dangers of climbing are real, but they can be controlled to a great extent by the use of proper techniques and modern equipment.

It is not the intention of this guidebook to remove the element of adventure from your Seneca visits, reduce the need for expertise on your part, or diminish the importance of personal responsibility. No guidebook is perfect—in this one, despite our best efforts, you may discover errors in pitch length, route descriptions, grades, and the like. To protect yourself, the editor strongly recommends that you:

- Consult with local climbers and frequent visitors for route information when needed.

- Seek qualified professional instruction when appropriate.

- Be aware that fixed protection (especially old pitons) may be dangerous.

- Review all of the information on safety found in these pages.

The first-time Seneca climber should be familiar with some of the potential hazards that may be encountered. Most hazards found at Seneca are the same as those experienced in many climbing areas throughout the world: unprotected routes, route finding problems, occasional loose holds, and rubble covered ledges. The following hazards warrant special attention:

1. Getting to the base of your route may require exposed scrambling. We recommend that all Seneca climbers have knowledge of roped fourth class climbing techniques.

2. Many harder routes at Seneca require placing small nuts from difficult and strenuous stances. Seneca climbing often requires the use of a large rack including slings of various lengths. Double ropes can be very useful.

3. Despite the overall excellent quality of the rock, Seneca surprises the climber with occasional loose holds and many debris-strewn ledges. The editors have had very few holds break in many years of climbing at Seneca, but have experienced several that moved under body weight. Rubble covered ledges present a serious rockfall hazard to climbers below and require utmost caution.

4. Some areas of the rock have been subject to rare but significant natural rockfall. Two recent examples are the fall of the Gendarme in 1987, and in 1972 the collapse of the entire upper Thais Face.

5. Seneca lies in a north-south orientation, putting the cliff directly in the path of the prevailing winds. Those winds can become fierce, especially along the South End, the Gunsight, the entire summit ridge of the South Peak, and in the major gaps. On windy days it is not uncommon to see ropes picked up by the wind and lifted high in the air.

6. An occasionally serious problem that may at first appear trivial are Seneca's pigeons. Several near disastrous incidents have occurred when roosting pigeons were startled by climbers scrambling near the summit. A speeding pigeon roaring past your head when you're unroped with a couple hundred feet of exposure under your feet can be frightening!

EMERGENCIES

If you are involved in a life-threatening emergency at Seneca it is important to initiate a careful evacuation to the road as quickly and safely as possible.

Rescue Gear and Services
Finding assistance for a rescue may be problematic at Seneca. The cliff is located in a remote area with only a small resident climbing population, and as of 1994 there was no official rescue entity at Seneca. If you are climbing mid-week or anytime in the off season, be prepared to carry out a self-rescue. If possible, send someone down to the town to contact climbing shop, guide service and local emergency medical personnel. The cliff is a half hour by highway from the nearest hospital. On several occasions victims of serious accidents have been evacuated by helicopter.

Rescue personnel may be found at The Gendarme climbing store, local climbing schools, and the fire and rescue service (304) 567-2412. A rescue cache is located on the front porch of The Gendarme climbing store. The cache includes basic equipment and a stokes litter. Climbers are urged to get first aid training and carry first aid kits.

Ambulance Service
Call (304) 567-2412 for ambulance service. If emergency evacuation is required from the vicinity of the rocks it may be possible to drive an emergency vehicle over the concrete low-water bridge at the end of Roy Gap Road. This road cannot be used if the river covers the bridge.

Hospitals
There are two hospitals in the area. The closest is Grant Memorial, (304) 257-1026, in Petersburg, 23 miles to the north on Rt. 55. A somewhat larger hospital, Davis Memorial, (304) 636-3300, is located in Elkins, about 40 miles west on Rt. 33.

NATURE OF SENECA ROCKS CLIMBS

The major cliffs of eastern West Virginia, which include Seneca, Champe, and Nelson Rocks, differ significantly from other eastern climbing areas. The rock is similar to the quartzite found in the Shawangunks of New York state, Pennsylvania and Maryland. In the Seneca area, the rock was subject to tremendous geological forces that literally tilted the entire strata on end. Seneca is a jagged group of towering fins whose South End resembles a fantastic cathedral with its many arches and buttresses.

If you like climbing dead vertical rock you'll love Seneca. Routes vary from one to four pitches, depending on the location. Almost all routes tend to be strenuous regardless of the length. Some climbs follow obvious lines while others wander up blank looking, vertical faces. Despite the steepness of the rock many moderate routes exist, due in part to the presence of larger cracks and holds.

LOCATION

The rocks are located in Pendleton County, West Virginia within sight of the cross-roads village of Seneca Rocks. The village is built around the intersection of routes 55, 33 and 28 in a remote area of the Allegheny Mountains, hours from the closest large city.

The area is extremely mountainous with narrow twisting highways. This beautiful, isolated region is just beginning to be discovered by large numbers of tourists. When planning your trip remember that the mountain ridges run generally north to south. Any roads that cut across the grain of the mountains tend to be more twisting and difficult to drive. In addition, remember that winter snowfall can be very heavy, making the trip potentially hazardous as well as slow.

Listed below are some suggested routes from different parts of the eastern United States:

Pittsburgh/Ohio cities: Take I-77 into West Virginia. Follow Rt. 33 east through Elkins to Seneca Rocks.

Philadelphia: Take I-76 west to I-81 south. Exit onto Rt. 55 west. Follow Rt. 55 west through Moorefield and Petersburg, WV and from there to Seneca.

Washington DC/Baltimore: Take Rt. 66 west to I-81 south. Follow I-81 south a short distance to Rt. 55 at Strasburg. Follow 55 west through Moorefield and Petersburg, WV and from there to Seneca.

Southern Virginia: Follow I-81 north to Harrisonburg, VA. Take Rt. 33 west to Seneca Rocks. A scenic alternative is via Rt. 220 north. Take I-81 to Rt. 220 just north of Roanoke. In Franklin, WV take Rt. 33 west to Seneca Rocks.

USING THE GUIDE

The main strength of this guide lies in the written descriptions of each climb and major rappel route. Photographs with lines provide orientation on a large scale and in many instances help identify the location of routes. Not all routes are marked on the photographs. Pitch lengths and other measurements may not be precise, but they are usually reasonably close.

This guide takes advantage of Seneca's north-south orientation. To orient yourself, remember that the West Face is the face seen from the village. While looking at the cliff from the Village, south is to your right and north to your left. All left and right directions are given with the assumption that you are facing the rock. Routes are described left to right for the South End, East Faces of both peaks, and Lower Slabs. Routes are described right to left for the West Faces of both peaks, and for the Southern Pillar.

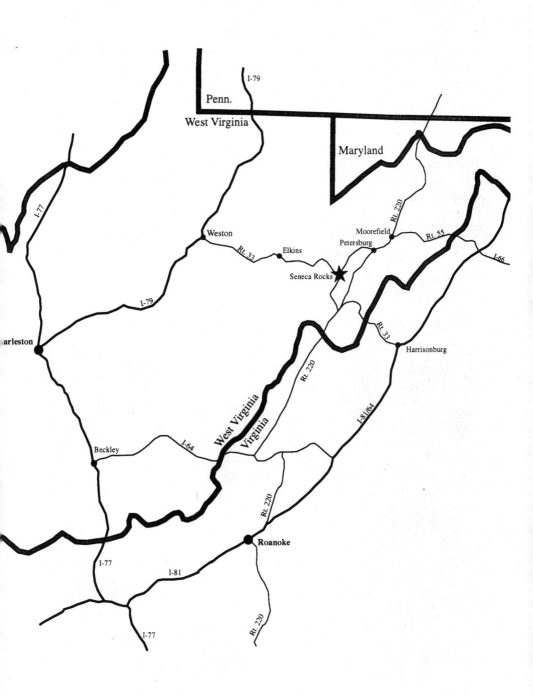

Highly recommended routes are identified by a single star (*). Many routes without a (*) are good. If a route is poor or unremarkable it usually looks it.

In order to climb safely and efficiently on this complex rock, it is wise to first learn as many of the different features as possible. Most of Seneca's major features are indicated on the various photographs that appear throughout the guide.

ACCESS

The best access to the rock is via the new pedestrian bridge at the temporary U.S. Forest Service Visitor's Center. After crossing the bridge, the trail forks. Take the left fork to access the north end of the Lower Slabs (see map) and the North Peak-East Face. Access all other faces via the right hand fork. This trail leads to Roy Gap Road and trailheads. The low water bridge on Roy Gap Road can also be used to cross the North Fork, as well as to bring vehicles into Roy Gap IN EMERGENCIES ONLY. Blue triangle blazes mark trails to both the east and west faces. Remember that bush-whacking and switchback cutting damage the rocky and friable soil. Soil washed down from the upper slopes of Seneca is gone for good.

A bird's eye-view of the town of Seneca Rocks

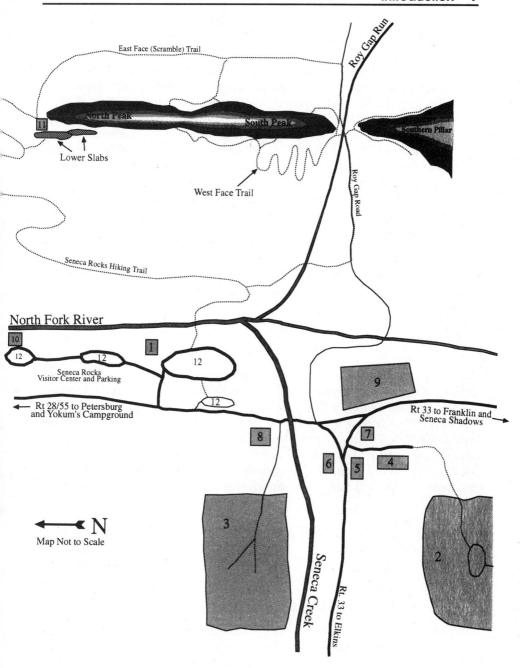

East Face (Scramble) Trail

Roy Gap Run

North Peak

South Peak

Southern Pillar

Lower Slabs

West Face Trail

Roy Gap Road

Seneca Rocks Hiking Trail

North Fork River

10

12

12

1

12

Seneca Rocks
Visitor Center and Parking

12

9

Rt 28/55 to Petersburg
and Yokum's Campground

Rt 33 to Franklin and
Seneca Shadows

8

7

6

5

4

11

3

2

Seneca Creek

Rt. 33 to Elkins

◄━━◄ N

Map Not to Scale

1. Temporary Visitor's Center
2. Seneca Shadows Campground
3. Princess Snowbird Campground
4. Gendarme/Seneca Rocks Climbing School
5. Harper's General Store
6. Seneca Rocks Mountain Guides & Outfitters

7. Yokum's Store
8. Post Office
9. Site of Future Visitor's Center
10. Swimming Hole
11. North Peak Observation Deck
12. Parking

DESCENT ROUTES

Part of the charm of Seneca is the almost alpine feeling one can get while climbing on the isolated summit. Seneca's alpine nature can also contribute to problems in organizing descents. Unlike most eastern rock climbing areas, the upper South Peak of Seneca (terrain above the level of Luncheon and Broadway ledges) requires rappelling to descend. Ropes of 165 feet or longer are required on some routes and are highly recommended for every descent. Major descent routes are described at the beginning of each section of the guide, and are also indicated by downward arrows on various photographs throughout the guide.

New drilled anchors have replaced many of the old rappel and belay stations, including dangerous old pitons and damaged trees. These new anchors facilitate descents, help prevent further erosion on commonly used descent routes, and protect trees growing in already stressful environments. Placing these anchors was a time-consuming and expensive task. Please assist in the effort by placing a contribution in the anchor donation box located in The Gendarme.

RATING SYSTEM

The greatest controversy in editing the 1990 version of this book revolved around Seneca's route difficulty rating system. Many individuals, especially those with long associations with Seneca, argued that the old Seneca rating system was a tradition that should be preserved. Another group, just as vocal, argued that Seneca's climbs were severely underrated compared to most areas in the United States. Worse, they argued, there seemed to be a lack of consistency in the ratings of the harder routes. These arguments had been debated for many years; however, for the first time, the argument for upgrading many of Seneca's routes seemed the loudest and most insistent.

One responsibility of a guide book editor is to respect the consensus opinions of the climbing community as well as uphold the traditions of the area he or she writes about. The editor must observe and record changes in the community's attitudes. The tide seemed to shift by 1990, and in response, so did many of the ratings that appear in this book.

This book uses the American Decimal System (ADS) (a.k.a. Yosemite Decimal System and Tahquitz Decimal System) in all its free climbing ratings. All climbers, but especially those new to the sport, should realize that this system is not perfect. All ratings are somewhat arbitrary and subjective in nature. Although efforts have been made to bring Seneca's ratings in line with the rest of the United States, the editors of this guide continue to advise that all visitors begin their first Seneca trip by climbing at least a grade lower than normal until a feel for Seneca ratings can be gained.

The ADS is burdened with the mistakes of its creators. The original system was originally conceived to end at 5.10. For many years the hardmen of the 1960s and 1970s placed harder and harder climbs in the "final" 5.10 level. Eventually someone recognized that a 5.11 grade would have to be created, but by then the damage was done. Instead of a logical system that would top out today at around 5.20, we now have fine delineation's of routes in the 5.10 range and harder. These delineation's are a, b, c, and d. For example a 5.10b is somewhat more difficult than a 5.10a.

The ADS system is straightforward (see chart below). The rating system is further enhanced by the addition of a protection rating system. It is important to note that the protection ratings tend to be even more subjective than the difficulty ratings.

DIFFICULTY RATINGS

5.0-5.2	Very Easy
5.3-5.5	Easy
5.6-5.8	Moderate
5.9-5.11	Difficult
5.12-5.13	Extremely Difficult

PROTECTION RATINGS

"R"   - Long runouts on easy to moderate rock with no protection, or dubious protection on shorter stretches of difficult rock. In the event of a fall there is significant danger of injury or death.

"X" - No protection over long stretches of difficult rock. A fall would most likely result in serious injury or death.

RECOMMENDED ROUTES

* - This symbol indicates a quality climb that is highly recommended.

FIRST ASCENT ETHICS

A few years ago the Seneca climbing community embraced one of the strongest no-bolts climbing ethics in the United States. In 1980 there were fewer than ten bolts on the entire cliff; each and every one of which was hotly debated long before they were placed, on the lead. The American bolting ethic has loosened considerably during the 1980s and early 1990s, but at Seneca their use continues to be sparse.

The related ethics of traditional clean climbing and environmental protection are crucial to the future of climbing at Seneca and elsewhere. A modern "traditional" ethic no longer means no bolts at all. With clean (or free pro) routes all but exhausted, bolting from hooks has sustained the spirit of adventure and opened new lines.

Seneca has always been an essentially traditional climbing area—the vast majority of climbs here are protected cleanly. A sense of proportion and an appreciation of tradition in the use of bolts comprises only one ingredient in our efforts to retain both access and a quality experience.

Aspiring first ascensionists at Seneca should bear in mind two things:

1. Many blank sections of face climbing around the rocks have been top-roped (TR) and thus exist as climbs, but are not listed in this guide. Some of the more obvious TR problems are cited in route descriptions of adjacent climbs.

2. The practice of drilling on the lead from stances and off hooks is now accepted at Seneca. For example, the difficult HEAVY FUEL (12c), was drilled from hooks.

ENVIRONMENT

The public perception that the climbing community abuses the environment is the most important issue facing the sport today. Climbers must act in a responsible manner to maintain climbing privileges on public property and must be proactive in promoting the truth concerning the sport's true environmental impact.

The most serious environmental problem at Seneca is that of erosion caused by climbers shortcutting trails or using alternative trails to reach the rocks. The rock sits on top of a very steep hill which has thin, rocky soils. Every person who cuts a switchback or uses one of the "unofficial" trails in order to save a few minutes on the approach or descent contributes to a problem which grows in magnitude every year.

The environmental impact of climbing can be reduced if everyone would try to do the following:

- Avoid disturbing plants and animals found on the approach and on the cliff.
- Plan your bowel movements for proper facilities in the valley.
- Carry out all litter, including old tape and cigarette butts.
- Avoid using trees for rappel anchors, if possible.
- Carpool to the rock.

Contributing money to The Access Fund, a non-profit organization devoted to preserving and attaining access to climbing areas, is an excellent way to support the environmentally sound ideas promoted by this group.

...Preserving America's diverse climbing resources.

The **Access Fund,** a national, non-profit climbers organization, is working to keep you climbing. The **Access Fund** works to preserve access and protect the environment by buying land, funding climber-support facilities, financing scientific studies, helping develop land management policy, publishing educational materials, and providing resources to local climbers' coalitions.

Every climber can help preserve access!!

- **Commit yourself to "leaving no trace."**
    Remove litter, old slings, etc. from campgrounds and the crags.
- **Dispose of human waste properly.**
    Use toilets whenever possible. If none are available, dig a hole at least 50 meters from water and bury waste. *Always pack out toilet paper* (use zip-lock plastic bags).
- **Use existing trails.**
    Avoid cutting switchbacks and trampling vegetation.
- **Use discretion when placing bolts & "fixed" protection.**
    Camouflage all anchors.
- **Respect restrictions to protect natural resources & cultural artifacts.**
    Be aware of seasonal closures to protect nesting raptors.
    Power drills are illegal in wilderness areas.
    Never chisel or sculpt holds in rock on public lands.
- **Park in designated areas.**
    Try not to park in undeveloped, vegetated areas.
- **Maintain a low profile.**
- **Respect private property.**
- **Join or form a group to deal with access issues in your area.**
    Consider sponsoring "clean-ups" and other events which promote access.
- **Join the Access Fund.**
    To join, simply make a tax-deductible donation of any amount.

The Access Fund • PO Box 17010 • Boulder, CO 80308

SERVICES

The nearest towns of significant size are Petersburg, about 25 minutes by road to the north on Rt. 28/55, Elkins, approximately 45 minutes to the west on Rt. 33, and the county seat of Franklin, 45 minutes south on Rt. 33. Canaan Valley (a resort area best known for skiing), and the town of Davis are approximately forty minutes to the northeast. All have basic services; Petersburg has the closest big grocery store and Elkins (a college town) and Davis are your best bets for entertainment.

Climbing Supplies and Climbing School/Guide Services
These friendly, professional outfits are great places to hang out or meet other climbers.

The Gendarme/Seneca Rocks Climbing School: The Gendarme (behind Harper's Store) is one of the oldest technical climbing shops in the east and is the home of Seneca Rocks Climbing School. The Gendarme and SRCS may be reached by telephoning (800) 548-0108 or (304) 567-2600.

Seneca Rocks Mountain Guides and Outfitters: Seneca Rocks Mountain Guides are located across the street from Harper's Store and can be reached by calling (800) 451-5108 from eastern states. Persons living in the western U.S. can call (304) 567-2115.

Camping
The great flood of 1985 destroyed the old U.S. Forest Service camping area along Roy Gap Road. A very comfortable Forest Service campground has been built in another location. There are two commercial campgrounds in the immediate area and great primitive camping in the surrounding Monongahela National Forest outside the Seneca Rocks portion of the Spruce Knob/Seneca Rocks National Recreation Area. Camping is not allowed on the rocks side of the North Fork River. Prices listed below were current in 1994.

Seneca Shadows - The new U.S. Forest Service campground is situated on a hill over-looking the town of Seneca Rocks. The entrance is located off Rt. 28, 1 mile south of the crossroads. Campground fees are: $7.00 per night for walk-in tent sites; $10.00 per night for single vehicle drive-in sites; $12.00 for drive-in sites with electrical hookup; $15.00 for double vehicle drive-in sites; $18.00 for double drive-in sites with electric hookups; $30.00 for drive-in group sites (with hookup). Reservations: 1-800-280-CAMP.

Yokum's Vacationland Campground - This campground is located about a half mile north of the crossroads on Rt. 55. Showers are available. The fee is $5.00 per person per night for drive-in sites with no hookup; $12.50 for tents and pop-ups at sites with hookups (two people; $2.00 per additional person over 6 years old); $13.50 for campers and RV trailers at hookup sites (two people; $2.00 per person for additional people over 6 years old). Reservations: 1-304-567-2351.

Princess Snowbird Campground - This is the old pavilion camping area previously owned by the now deceased Buck Harper. Carl and Shirley Yokum now operate this camping area which is located behind the Post Office, along Seneca Creek. This is the closest camping to the rocks and the same rates apply as for Yokum's Vacationland. Cabins and ersatz Indian teepees are also available. Reservations: 1-304-567-2351.

Motels

There are two motels in the vicinity.

Yokum's Motel/Cabins- (304) 567-2351, is located about half a mile north of the crossroads on Rt. 55.

4-U motel- (304) 567-2111, located about 2 miles south of the crossroads on Rt. 55.

In addition, there are several motels 23 miles north of Seneca in the town of Petersburg.

Groceries and Supplies

Food and other supplies can be purchased at Harper's Country Store and Yokum's Grocery, the two general stores that are located at the crossroads.

Restaurants

4-U: Located about 2 miles south of the crossroads on Rt. 55. Traditional American diner style that serves breakfast, lunch and dinner.

Front Porch: Located directly above Harper's Country Store, next to the Gendarme. The restaurant serves lunch and dinner and specializes in pizza and sandwiches. Please don't bring beer to the restaurant or the front porch of Harper's store.

Yokum's: Located about half a mile north of the crossroads on Rt. 55. The restaurant serves traditional American diner style for breakfast, lunch, and dinner.

Valley View: Drive 5 miles south on Rt. 55. Traditional American diner style open for breakfast, lunch, and dinner.

U.S. Forest Service Visitor Center

Particularly attractive on a rainy day, the temporary visitor's center offers informative displays, maps, books, and regular film and video shows. The new visitor's center is tentatively scheduled for completion in 1996. The location is proposed to be 250 yards south of the steel footbridge.

Drinking Water

Potable water can be obtained from taps in the Forest Service Seneca Shadows campground facilities, and from a spigot behind the temporary Visitor Center rest rooms (this last source may be located elsewhere with the completion of the permanent new Center).

Swimming

The Forest Service swimming area is located about half a mile north of the Visitor Center. A trail leads to the river from the last parking lot.

Showers

Showers can be obtained for a small fee at Yokum's Vacationland Campground and the Princess Snowbird Campground. Seneca Shadows Campground has showers for guests.

HISTORY

This rugged area of eastern West Virginia has been influenced by many diverse cultures: primitive Indians, modern Indian tribes, escaped indentured servants, European settlers of the colonial era, and the present day residents that live and work the valleys.

The first settlers were Indians. Some evidence indicates that very primitive Indians from the Archaic Era may have camped at the mouth of Seneca Creek. Although some permanent Indian settlement took place in this area of West Virginia, the Seneca area was primarily used by various tribes for travel and as a hunting ground. The famous Seneca Trail followed the Potomac River, allowing the Algonquin, Tuscarora, and Seneca tribes to trade and make war on each other. As the Indians moved along the trail they must have used the prominent rocks of Champe and Seneca as landmarks. The local legend of Princess Snowbird may be derived from the presence of a band of Seneca Indians which once lived in the area—or it may be the romantic fantasy of later occupants of European descent. While the Indians must have had thousands of years of very fascinating experiences, their lack of recorded history makes knowledge of that time relatively sparse.

The first European settlers to the region appeared about the year 1746. At that time, West Virginia, then part of what is now Virginia, was the fringe of the great unknown, the American wilderness. The first settlers were preceded by a few mountain men and escaped indentured servants running from Virginia plantations. As time went on, the wilderness rapidly receded to the west.

The American Revolution affected the region as its citizens became embroiled in the conflict and some residents died in the fighting. Various Indian raids slowed development of the region, and on occasion, the European settlers retreated before the Indian attacks. By the time of the Civil War, the Indians had long been driven out of the area.

The Civil War era proved difficult for the residents of Pendleton County. The common belief that the Civil War split families apart was generally true only in border state regions such as Pendleton County. A little over half the county residents were southern sympathizers, the rest were loyal to the north. In this county brother did fight brother, neighbors became enemies, and people were ambushed and killed because of their politics. At the conclusion of the war, the state of West Virginia was carved from Virginia and the residents of the Seneca region returned to a slow and settled rural lifestyle.

CLIMBING HISTORY

The climbing history of Seneca remains undocumented prior to the year 1939, however it has been argued that Indians may have climbed the South Peak prior to the coming of the European settlers. An early ascent by Indians may have happened; although most evidence from other peaks throughout the United States suggests that these ancient peoples were not greatly interested in climbing difficult summits. It is possible, and maybe probable, that Indians climbed the South Peak of Seneca, but if this occurred it is unlikely that any evidence will ever surface to verify such an ascent. If Indians failed to reach the summit, it is likely that some European settler devised a method of reaching the top of the South Peak. With settlers living almost in the shadow of the cliff it seems reasonable that some young farmer or tradesman must have explored the cliff to the extent necessary to find one of the easier routes to the top.

The first known ascent appears to have taken place in the year 1908. When Paul Bradt, Don Hubbard, and Sam Moore were making their historic 1939 ascent, they discovered an inscription carved on the summit rock: "D.B. Sept. 16, 1908". It is probable that the inscription was left by a surveyor named Bittenger who worked in the region at that time. The editor of this guide has difficulty believing that Seneca was unclimbed until 1908. However until additional evidence surfaces, it must be assumed that "D.B." was the first person to reach the summit of the South Peak.

In the years between 1908 and 1939 climbers made several attempts on Seneca walls. The late Mr. Buck Harper reported that several parties armed with climbing equipment made attempts on the cliff. However, he did not know if they were successful or what routes they attempted. He mentioned that his father had made an attempt on the summit during that period. On another occasion a local "bandit" attempted to topple the Gendarme (known to local residents as the Chimney) with explosives.

The documented climbing history of Seneca Rocks began in 1935 with a roped descent of the North Peak by Paul Bradt and Florence Perry. Paul Bradt, Janet Mabry, and Bob Gleichman returned in 1938 and worked out a route into the Gunsight from the north side of the rock.

A long Easter weekend in 1939 gave Paul Bradt, Don Hubbard, and Sam Moore the opportunity they needed to climb to the South Peak via an inspired traverse. Their route took in what today are considered many separate climbs and parts of climbs. The group did this ambitious ascent with only 3 carabiners. Their route took two days to accomplish and followed today's LOWER SKYLINE DIRECT, the last 2 pitches of SKYLINE TRAVERSE, COCKSCOMB CHIMNEY, the second pitch of WINDY

Paul Bradt, Sam Moore, Donald Hubbard on the South Peak Summitt. 1939.   Photo: Paul Bradt.   Print: John Meenahan

Paul Bradt on the South Peak of Seneca,
(Photo: Don Hubbard. Print: John Meenehan.)

CORNER, and then on up to the summit. From the summit they downclimbed to the north as far as they could, then rappelled the East Face. The rappel placed them to the south of the Gunsight in the fading light. Their adventure was capped by a pendulum into the Gunsight followed by a lengthy scramble through the woods. On the way down they met a rescue party racing to save them. They named the entire route SKY-LINE TRAVERSE.

After doing GUNSIGHT NOTCH EAST with Jim Lamb in September of 1939, the trio returned in 1940 to record several more first ascents. On this trip they climbed the now fallen GENDARME, GUNSIGHT TO SOUTH PEAK, and a descent of OLD LADIES' ROUTE. The method used for the ascent of the GENDARME is particularly interesting. They repeatedly threw a rope over the top of the pinnacle until it finally caught, creating a toprope situation. They belayed on the west side of the Gendarme and climbed on the east side. Bradt reported the climb to be extremely difficult until Hubbard found an easy line. On Labor Day weekend, 1940, Bradt used the easier line to lead to the top of the pinnacle with Bill Kemper in tow.

During the early 1940s climbers began a slow but steady exploration of the cliff. Prior to World War II, the hardcore Seneca regulars came from either the Washington D.C. area or from Pittsburgh. The Washington climbers were associated with the Potomac Appalachian Trail Club (PATC); the majority of the Pittsburgh climbers were members of either the Pittsburgh Explorers Club, led by Ivan Jirak, or a group known as the Pittsburgh Social Climbers, led by Sayre Rodman.

The sport was far different in its infancy than it is today. Herb Conn, an early Seneca climber estimates that fewer than 30 climbers a year visited the rocks in the years immediately preceding the war. Travel was difficult and gear scarce. Older Seneca climbers report that in the early 1940s only 3 carabiners existed in the entire city of Washington D.C.. Climbing teams would seek out easier sections of rock and wander where they could. Prior to the war, routes were not named or rated. An interesting fact was that the majority of the PATC climbers worked for the same employer; most were scientists working with the U.S. Bureau of Standards. The climbers of the 1940s were not like the climbing athletes of today. Climbers were considered odd by most people. Few of the practitioners ever worked out or trained for the sport, beyond an occasional practice session at nearby Carderock or Great Falls.

During the war years only a few climbers managed to visit the rocks due to the difficulties created by the war. Government employees worked 5 1\2 days a week, and gasoline rationing prevented travel to the distant Seneca area. Some made the trip on occasion by filling an automobile with climbers and making the drive on long weekends. In 1943-44 the U.S. Army used Seneca to train mountain troops for action in the Apennines. The 10th Mountain Division held a 2 week training camp and taught such useful mountaineering tactics as aid climbing using silent signals and muffled piton hammers. The skills learned by these men were actually used in combat when the U.S. Army's 10th Division launched a night attack on an exposed Italian ridge, achieving total surprise. Decayed ring angle pitons from their training activities still pepper various routes at Seneca and elsewhere along the North Fork Valley. During

Don Hubbard on OLD LADIES ROUTE. (Photo: Paul Bradt. Print: John Meenehan)

their stay the army drove over 75,000 pitons into the cliffs of Seneca, Champe, and Nelson rocks. Unfortunately, many of the army routes were never recorded and have since been renamed. Although most of the army's routes have passed out of memory, they are still noted for two of Seneca's most popular routes, CONN'S WEST and CONN'S EAST.

The 1940s ended with a resurgence of climbing at Seneca. Climbers suddenly found themselves rich with equipment. Army carabiners could be obtained from surplus supplies. Prototype army nylon ropes, obtained from friends employed by the Defense Department, replaced the old heavy 7\16" hemp ropes used by climbers for decades. The climbers of the time used thousands of free pitons left behind by the troops. They simply pounded out the pins as needed. Climbers of the late 1940s tended to repeat many of the army routes and often followed lines of fixed pitons up the side of the cliff. The Explorers Club of Pittsburgh prepared the first climbers' guidebook during this period, merely a list of climbs at the rock.

Paul Bradt was probably the first real "hardman" at Seneca. He became a motivating force among the Washington D.C. climbers. Using techniques he learned from "Gus" Gambs, a Frenchman employed by the State Department, Bradt climbed many of the first routes at Seneca, Champe and other rocks. He was also a great caver. He led the first expeditions into the famous Schoolhouse Cave, only a few miles from Seneca. This cave was considered the most difficult cave in the United States for many years. Even today, Schoolhouse is a serious challenge deserving respect. Don Hubbard was another star of the era. Arnold Wexler, a contemporary of Hubbard described him as a "fantastic climber" who constantly downplayed his own abilities. Hubbard so often stated that he was too old to climb, that Jan Conn wrote a song in 1940 poking fun at the supposedly aging warrior. Hubbard made his last Seneca climb in 1983 at the age of 83. On that trip he summited the South Peak and the Gendarme.

The climbers of the 1940s, those pioneers that built on the early achievement of Bradt, Moore, and Hubbard, were considered people with an odd passion. Paul Bradt, Herb and Jan Conn, Charlie Daniels, Don Hubbard, Andy Kauffman, Sam Moore, Chris Scordoes, and others broke the ice at Seneca. Of the core group, only Andy Kauffman and the Conns would go on to receive any degree of fame. Kauffman was known for his mountaineering exploits and the Conns for their many early first ascents all over the United States.

The fifties and early sixties were dominated by climbers such as John Christian, Sayre Rodman, Jim Shipley, Tony Soler, Arnold Wexler, and others. These climbers increased the quantity and quality of Seneca routes. Some of their better efforts include GREEN WALL, MARSHALL'S MADNESS, SOLER and TRIPLE S. The ascent of the classic TRIPLE S was notable. Shipley led the steep corner with pitons generally too small for the crack. Perhaps the best climber of the 1950s was Tony Soler. His SOLER ROUTE was incredibly bold for the time. The climb ascends the East Face at its highest point and ends with an exposed traverse to a hidden ledge.

In the late 1960s the number of climbers active at Seneca greatly increased. As more and more climbers made their mark, the number of difficult routes rose tremendously. The climbers of this period had the advantage of better equipment and improved techniques. In addition, competition began to appear at Seneca as a motivating force. These factors allowed the leaders of the Seneca climbing community to concentrate on the creation of hard free climbs. Matt Hale was one of the leaders of this movement. He led the first free ascents of COTTONMOUTH and AGONY. George Livingstone put up the first Seneca route ever given the grade of 5.10 with his lead of MADMEN ONLY (5.10b/c). COTTONMOUTH and AGONY were both later upgraded to .10a and .10b respectively. Other leaders of the era include Tom Evans, Barry Walden, and Bob Lyon.

The 1970s continued the trend of more and harder routes that began in the late 1960s. In 1971 Pat Milligan and George Livingstone did the twin cracks of CASTOR and POLLUX. John Stannard freed TOTEM, and gave Seneca its first 5.11. As the decade progressed a new crowd began to flex its muscles. The prolific Herb Laeger, most often assisted by Eve Uiga managed a long list of hard climbs including CLIMBIN' PUNISHMENT, RIGHT TOPE, HIGH TEST, NIP AND TUCK, and TERRA FIRMA HOMESICK BLUES. Other hardmen of the period included Howard Doyle and Eric Janoscrat, who began climbing many poorly protected natural lines. Marty McLaughlin, Leith Wain, Ray Snead, Jeff Burns, Hunt Prothro, and Jessie Guthrie also contributed greatly to the first ascent scene. Ray Snead, John Stannard, and others who were active in past years continued to assist in the development of the area.

The 1980s were an unusually turbulent decade for Seneca. The Seneca community suffered three setbacks: the death of Buck Harper, the fall of the Gendarme, and the great flood of 1985.

Buck Harper, the owner of the Harper General Store and friend to many climbers died at the age of 74. Mr. Harper was a familiar figure in his bib overalls. At first impression he seemed to be a man that would not inspire friendship from visiting climbers. He often spit tobacco in the general direction of a paint can placed against the stove in his store. Another game that Buck liked to play was "punch me in the stomach". He offered to let climbers hit him in the stomach as hard as they wanted if he could return the favor. He played this game well into his 70s. These antics did not hide the fact that he was an intelligent man who loved to debate the members of the generally more liberal climbing community. His death was a shock to the dozens of climbers who visited Buck's store for many years.

On October 22, 1987, at 3:27 p.m., the Gendarme fell: an event recorded in numerous outdoor magazines. Prior to appearing in print, news of the fall flashed across the country by word of mouth. Someone not familiar with Seneca might wonder at the nationwide attention given to the demise of this little pinnacle. The Gendarme was a special climb. Terribly exposed, it leaned out over the west face. An easy, but airy, 5.4 route followed the east face of the pinnacle to a very tiny, pointed summit. Countless pilgrims arrived at the microscopic, sloping summit to find that vertigo would not allow them to stand up! Since 1940, when Bradt, Hubbard, and Perry made the first ascent, this 25 ft. blade of rock was one of Seneca's most popular climbs. Over the

Marian Harvey, Herb Conn, Jan Conn on the South Peak Summitt about 1950.
(Photo: Conn collection.)

Jack Wilson preparing to rappel from North Peak in 1939.
(Photo: Meenehan collection.)

years, thousands of people had climbed the narrow pinnacle and stood, or tried to stand, on its summit. No one ever doubted that the Gendarme would go someday, its deeply cracked base was much smaller than the rest of the pinnacle. The only important question was whether anyone would be on the summit when it toppled. Fortunately it happened on a weekday without casualties. The last known ascent was by local guide Tony Barnes and his client Charlie Reese on October 19, 1987.

On November 4, 1985 West Virginia suffered the worst night of flooding in its recorded history. In one night, the great flood of 1985 brought dramatic changes to the physical environment of the Seneca region. The record floodwaters killed dozens of people and caused millions of dollars in property loss. The losses to the climbing community were minor compared to the tragedies suffered by many local residents. However, some changes to the area stand out. The traditional climbers' camping area along Roy Gap Road was destroyed, as was the old swinging bridge. A bigger campground has been built and a much larger and safer bridge now spans the North Fork River. Time and money have repaired the physical damage to the Seneca area, but decades of tradition were swept away with the flood in November, 1985.

On the climbing front, the 1980s brought another change to the Seneca community. A gradual nationwide acquiescence to sport climbing methods in the United States turned into a tidal wave. Seneca has long held a reputation as a crag with many hard gear routes and sometimes difficult protection. At first it seemed improbable that these "Euro" methods would find acceptance at such a traditional area. Prior to 1984,

Don Hubbard (right) was on the first ascent of the Gendarme in 1939. Tony Barnes (left) made the last ascent in 1987. (Photo: Gendarme collection.)

The Gendarme before the fall.
(Photo: Bill Mohney.)

all routes were done from the ground up, including cleaning. After 1984, several hard routes were put up using such methods as rappel-placed bolts and pre-inspection. These routes are located on walls that would have been extremely difficult to climb using ground-up techniques. John Bercaw, one of Seneca's finest climbers, provides an ideal example of the changes that swept the area. In the September/October 1979 edition of CLIMBING magazine, Bercaw published an article entitled "What Price Glory?" In the article he lamented the "disease of impurism". The disease in Bercaw's mind seemed to be manifested by tactics commonly used today on first ascents in many climbing areas around the country.

Bercaw complained of "aid first tactics, toproping, or resting on protection". In the article he described the placement of Seneca's first bolt as a defacement of the cliff. Today several fine Bercaw routes, complete with bolts, are found at Seneca. The change in style and ethics at Seneca was tempered to a certain degree by strong tradition values. Most of the hard, new thin face climbs protected by bolts were drilled on the lead from hooks.

The 1980s brought many 5.12s and one 5.12d/.13a route, FINE YOUNG CANNI-BALS. One of the forces behind this movement toward extreme routes was the founding of the Seneca Rocks Climbing School. The owner of the School has consistently hired very talented climbers as instructors. These young tigers armed with the best modern gear, skill, and plenty of spare time put up many excellent hard routes. The activists of the 1980s, some of whom were local guides, included Cal Swoager, Paul Anikis, Howard Doyle, John Bercaw, Eric Janoscrat, Eddie Begoon, Pete Absolon, Mike Perliss, Greg Smith, Mike Cote, Mike Artz, Tom Cecil (now owner of Seneca Rocks Mountain Guides), and Darell Hensley.

In 1981 Cal Swoager completed Seneca's first 5.12 pitch when he freed the first pitch of SATISFACTION #1 (5.12c). John Bercaw introduced Seneca's first 5.13 in 1988, the continuation of Cal's line over the roof. John Bercaw called the completed route FINE YOUNG CANNIBALS. Cal Swoager also free climbed the fearsome BELL route on the North Peak. Both Jeff Burns and Bill Webster had taken falls in excess of 60 ft. while attempting to aid climb this line in the 1970s.

As the decade progressed, Seneca climbers developed the cliff in two ways; the creation of very hard free climbs with minimal and sometimes nonexistent gear, and the development of face climbs using some rappel but mostly hook placed bolts. Examples of the former include Cal Swoager's, THE BELL 5.12a R; Pete Absolon's, SUMMER'S EVE 5.10d X; and Greg Smith's, TOTAL MALFUNCTION 5.11c X. Climbs in the latter category include Eddie Begoon's and Mike Artz's MR. JONES 5.11c, John Bercaw's BROTHERS IN ARMS 5.12b, and the Bill Moore-Parker brothers creation THUNDERBOLTS 5.11d. The number of persons leading and putting up hard new lines was at an all time high.

The early 1990s saw continuing new route activity, most of it involving the use of bolts placed from aid, especially hooks, to which tiny, diamond-hard Seneca features lend themselves particularly well. Tom Cecil has been at the forefront of upholding the ground-up style, doing hard routes on the remaining faces. Eddie Begoon, Darell Hensley, and several others have also been hard at work.

In a sad development, the Forest Service Visitor Center building which had been standing since 1978 burned to the ground on May 26, 1992. It housed irreplaceable natural history specimens and records, as well as prized exhibits. A temporary building is in place, and a permanent replacement is scheduled to be completed by 1996. Rumors of arson flew shortly after the fire, but the fire marshal was unable to determine if vandalism was involved.

The rocks have seen generations come and go. The environment, the people, the traditions, and climbing styles have undergone many changes since climbing began at Seneca. The 1990's have already seen even more change as standards rise. The young tigers of today will someday look with awe on the accomplishments of those who follow. It has always been this way, and as long as climbing continues, it will probably remain so.

GEOLOGY

Eastern West Virginia contains many soaring crags of white/gray Tuscarora quartzite. Seneca, Nelson, Champe, and many other lesser rocks are made of the same rock as the famous cliffs of the Shawangunks in New York state. The quartzite is approximately 250 feet thick in West Virginia and is located primarily on exposed ridges as caprock or exposed crags. The rock is formed from sand grains deposited approximately 440 million years ago, in an extensive sheet at the edge of an ancient ocean. About 300 million years ago that ancient ocean was slowly destroyed by continental drift, as the area of eastern North America uplifted, thus forming the Appalachian mountains. These mountains were huge by today's standards, much larger than today's Himalayas. The active geological forces of the era threw the Tuscarora and other rock layers into great folds and zones of sheared rock. Far below the surface, one of the largest of these folds formed a miles wide arch in the Tuscarora.

Tens of millions of years of erosion stripped away the overlaying rock, including the dome of the Tuscarora arch. Fragments of the northwest wall of the arch remain as Seneca, Nelson, and Champe rocks. These rocks lie in a straight line northwest and southwest along North Fork Valley. The top and southeast slope of the arch are preserved on the skyline of North Fork Mountain, whose cliffs of Tuscarora quartzite are visible to the east from Seneca. The cliffs of Seneca remain because the rock is far harder than the surrounding rock. The vertical bedding of the cliff encourages sloughing off of layers, much like an onion. Seneca will be around for a long time but in the lifetime of the average climber some geologic changes can be seen.

CORRECTIONS AND REVISIONS

PLEASE SEND CORRECTIONS AND ADDITIONS TO:

Earthbound Sports Inc.
PO Box 3312
Chapel Hill, NC 27515-3312

Jeff Burns on POLLUX (5.10) in the late 1970's. He was killed in an accident on Teewinot in the Teton Range in 1980. (Photo: Bill Webster.)

THE SOUTHERN PILLAR

When viewing the rock from the valley, Seneca's twin peaks are clearly visible to the left of Roy Gap. The Southern Pillar is a series of long narrow buttresses and chimneys which rise from the hillside on the right side of the Gap. There is a concentration of good climbs (routes #6-33) in the Pillar's large, northwest-facing amphitheater. The amphitheater can be recognized by the numerous hemlock trees and small boulders which lie between the prow of the longest (GEPHART-DUFTY) buttress and a blocky wall with a shallow cave on the right wall. Other routes are located above and to the right of this central area, and on the east side of the Southern Pillar.

APPROACH

The hike to the best routes on the Southern Pillar is the shortest approach at Seneca. Take the climbers' access trail (the right fork after the bridge) to Roy Gap Road. Walk up Roy Gap Road to a large boulder on the right side of the road. On this boulder is a memorial plaque to Sneza Kelly, who died in a fall at Seneca in 1982. Just past the boulder and before the Roy Gap Run culvert, a trail cuts up and right through rocks and hemlock roots. GEPHART-DUFTY and SLIPSTREAM are the first routes reached. Routes #1-5 are best approached by skirting the base of the amphitheater wall, beginning at SLIPSTREAM and heading up and right. Routes #35-42 start on the east side of the Southern Pillar. Trails are marked with blue blazes.

It's fairly difficult to approach routes #1-5 and #35-43. Steep vegetated ramps on the right side of the amphitheater and a scree and dirt slope littered with deadfall on the left side lead to these outlying routes. The best approaches start on the marked trail and skirt the base of the formation.

DESCENT

The best descents, which allow you to avoid the nasty trail on the east side of the Pillar, are by rappel. The top of the Pillar has lots of loose rock; so be careful not to bomb those below. Rappel anchors can be found in the following locations:

- Locate anchors at the top of the original third pitch of CLIMBIN' PUNISH-MENT. It is 165 ft. to the ground from these, but note that rope snags are a definite hazard. Another set of cold shut anchors is 45 ft. below these, just right of ROY GAP CHIMNEYS at a ledge with a square block on it, and under a smooth roof. Fifty feet lower still is a tree with slings.

- There are also pairs of anchor bolts above SLIPSTREAM, RIGHT TOPE, BLOCK PARTY, BROWN BETTY and UP YOURS. Because the cold shuts above DAYTRIPPER also serve SLIPSTREAM they are located further left than the original top belay point.

If you top out on some long routes in the central area, such as CLIMBIN' PUNISH-MENT and ROY GAP CHIMNEYS, descend by scrambling down the steep, nasty east side trail.

Routes #1-5 are located on the small isolated buttress above and to the right of the aforementioned main amphitheater.

1 FEAR OF FLYING 5.7
Start about 25 ft. to the right of an arching, black and orange dihedral.
#1 Climb the chimney and right-facing corner to the overhang. Move left and up, then step back right into the crack system. Climb the cracks to the top. (100 ft.)
FA Rich Pleiss, Gene Genay 1975

2 THE VICTIM 5.7
Start just left of the dihedral mentioned in FEAR OF FLYING.
#1 Climb the face and crack, aiming for a squeeze chimney. Climb through the chimney and head straight to the top. (100 ft.)
FA Rich Pleiss, Gene Genay 1975

3 EXIT FROM THE VICTIM 5.4
(Var.) Climb the normal route until it is possible to step left 5 ft. to an easy corner. Follow the corner to the top. This variation avoids some bushwhacking at the top.

4 ROLLING ROCK 5.8
Scramble past the start of FEAR OF FLYING to the base of the smooth west-facing slab high on the cliff.
#1 Climb the loose wall to the right of the slab, aiming for a left-leaning groove. Climb left under the groove then up the face to easier rock. Continue up a left leaning cleft through the overhang. Up this to the top. (120 ft.)
FA Eric Janoscrat, Jim McAtee 1978
Take plenty of small wires for the climb and fortitude for the approach.

5 STONEYS 5.7
The start is the same as ROLLING ROCK.
#1 Climb the slab to its end. (70 ft.)
#2 Ascend the right wall to a corner. Follow the corner to a roof. Surmount the roof using cracks. Once above the roof climb the thin crack which splits the face. (120 ft.)
FA Eric Janoscrat, Jim McAtee 1978

Routes #6-37, which lie on the main rock mass close to the road, are easy to approach. The first of the routes described here begin on the right side of the low, loose-looking wall on the upper, far right side of the amphitheater.

6 THE LEMUR 5.5
Near the right (west) side of the rotten wall mentioned above is a corner. Begin 30 ft. left of the corner.
#1 Climb the vegetated face and angle left to a slightly overhanging wall. Belay at a large pine on the tree covered platform. Descend by rappelling. (65 ft.)
FA Eric Janoscrat, Len Sistek 1976

7   APPENDICITIS 5.7

About 55 ft. to the left of the west edge of the wall is a shallow cave. Start just right of the cave.

#1   Climb the wall up under the dihedral. Head left until it is possible to climb the wall to the left of the dihedral. (110 ft.)

FA Eric Janoscrat, Len Sistek 1976

8   UP YOURS 5.12a **R**

Start 15 ft. left of APPENDICITIS, in the right margin of the cave.

#1   Climb out of the shallow cave on blocky holds to better rock, then up the overhanging face to cold shuts. There are 6 bolts. (45 ft.)

FA Brian McCray 1993

Don't fall while trying to clip the second bolt!

9   BROWN BETTY 5.12d

Start just left of UP YOURS.

#1   Climb up and out of the deepest part of the cave, tending left. This route joins UP YOURS near the top. There are 5 bolts if you use the first and last bolts of UP YOURS. (45 ft.)

FA Brian McCray 1993

10   BORDER PATROL 5.11c **R/X**

Start 20 ft. left of BROWN BETTY, from the top of a blocky pedestal.

#1   Boulder up and right on light gray rock, past an ominous chunky flake and small left-facing corners, to a ledge.

FA Rob Robinson, Robyn Erbesfield 1984

This route was altered in 1989 after local climber Mike Artz fell after breaking several holds. He avoided injury on this dangerous route by placing gear in the adjacent BLOCK PARTY. The climb is not known to have had an ascent since this mishap.

11   BLOCK PARTY 5.8 *

At the point where the quality of the blocky wall begins to improve there are two steep crack and face climbs on orange rock. Start fifteen feet right of a slot-like cave in the amphitheater's corner and just left of BORDER PATROL.

#1 Climb left-facing corners to a ledge with cold shuts. (45 ft.) There are some loose holds.

#2 Go up and left past blocky grunge to a platform.

FA Matt Hale, Ray Snead 1975.

12   QUIT DOGGIN' THE SCENE 5.8+

Start about 90 ft. above the normal finish of BLOCK PARTY.

#1   Scramble to a sloping ledge below a large overhang. Climb the overhang to cracks in the center of the face. Continue up these to the top.

FA Greg Collins, George Flam 1981

13 AMBUSH 5.11a *
Begin a few feet left of BLOCK PARTY on orange rock.
#1 Climb the overhanging orange wall via square holds. Continue up a short hand crack and some painful fingerlocks. (40 ft.)
FA Howard Doyle, Eric Janoscrat, Marty McLaughlin 1979

14 POINT MAN 5.11b
Begin at the slot-like cave where the rotten wall meets the first large buttress. Start at the right side of the cave.
#1 Climb up the cave to the roof. Follow the crack through the roof and belay at the tree. (35 ft.)
FA Howard Doyle, Marty McLaughlin, Eric Janoscrat 1981

15 BIZARRE GRANDIOSE 5.9
Use the same start as POINT MAN.
#1 Climb the right side of the cave until it is possible to reach a flake on the left wall. Climb the flake then go straight up the corner to a ledge. (100 ft.)
FA Greg Collum, Ron Augustino 1975
A 5.8 variation can be climbed a few feet right of the normal crux.

16 ELECTRIC CHAIR 5.9
Use the same start as BIZARRE GRANDIOSE.
#1 Climb BIZARRE GRANDIOSE a short distance. Continue up the arete and discontinuous crack to a small hardwood tree with rappel slings. (70 ft.)
FA Ed Begoon, Darell Hensley 1986. Three bolts were added in 1993 by the first ascent party.

17 THE JUDGMENT SEAT 5.10a *
Use the same start as BIZARRE GRANDIOSE.
#1 Climb the first few feet of BIZARRE GRANDIOSE until it is possible to move up and left, following an undercling flake to a severely sloping ledge. Continue up a steep wall to a triangular chimney. Climb out the chimney and up a steep crack to a large ledge. (70 ft.)
#2 Move right and follow cracks until below a large smooth roof. Step right and continue up to the top. (145 ft.)
FA Jeff Burns, Bill Webster 1975

18 JUDGE NOT 5.9
Start between DISCO DEATH MARCH and JUDGMENT SEAT.
#1 Climb the face, just left of the blocky orange section, to the sloping ledge. (40 ft.)
#2 Continue up the face using the left-most crack system. Move left past a bolt to the left corner of the face. Pass the JUDGMENT SEAT alcove and move up and right onto the upper face. Follow a thin vertical crack left of JUDGMENT SEAT to the large ledge. (50 ft.)
FA Sean Cleary, Ashton Walton, John Wright 1989

19   DISCO DEATH MARCH 5.10b *

Start about 8 ft. right of ROY GAP CHIMNEYS and below the buttress.

#1   Move up the narrow north-facing wall to a vertical crack. Climb the crack in order to reach another crack which lies a few feet right of the small ROY GAP CHIMNEYS tree. Continue up the crack to a broken face. Climb the face for about 12 ft. to reach a small ledge. Move left into ROY GAP CHIMNEYS.

FA   Howard Doyle, Eric Janoscrat

A strenuous route with good protection.

20   D.D.M. DIRECT FINISH 5.10d

(Var.) Instead of moving left to the chimney continue straight up the arete.

FA   Ed Begoon, Howard Clark 1989

21 ROY GAP CHIMNEYS 5.6

Start under the obvious chimney on the right side of the west face of the main buttress.

#1 Climb up to the chimney, passing a small tree. Continue to blocks and belay. (80 ft.)

#2 Continue up the chimney to a good ledge on the right. (80 ft.)

#3 Continue up the chimney, then move right onto the buttress. Climb up a short corner to the top. (40 ft.)

FA Tom McCrum, Roger Birch April 1969

22 CLIMBIN' PUNISHMENT 5.9+ *

Begin just left of the chimney at a dihedral with a ramp at its base and a smooth left wall.

#1 Climb the dihedral to a small ledge on the left (This is an optional belay if desired). Continue up the beautiful corner, past small overhangs to a lower angled ramp. (120 ft.)

#2 Climb to the roof and pass it on the left. Continue up past bulges to cold shut anchors on the left wall. (70 ft.)

#3 After a short scramble up and left, climb the small crack that splits the west face of the buttress. (40 ft.)

FA Herb Laeger, Mike Goff

Many parties avoid the last pitch, which is hard to protect. The first two pitches make an excellent 5.8 route.

23 RIGHT TOPE 5.9 *

Start about 20 ft. left of ROY GAP CHIMNEYS and 10 ft. left of CLIMBIN' PUNISHMENT, below a small inside corner.

#1 Climb the crack about 40 ft. to a small overhang. Move past the overhang by climbing the face on the right side of the crack. Continue up the flake past another overhang. Belay at cold shuts. (95 ft.)

#2-3 Climb easier rock to the top.

FA Herb Laeger, Eve Uiga

24 TIGHT ROPE 5.9

(Var.) Instead of climbing the undercling/lieback crux of RIGHT TOPE, follow a flake up and right, to a thin crack and face with a bolt. Belay at a tree. (100 ft.)

FA Darrell Hensley, Sandy Fleming, Dave McCutcheon 1993

25 SWEET RELEASE 5.12a

Start just left of RIGHT TOPE. Move up a left-facing corner. Angle up and left to a sloping ledge and clip a bolt. Go up to a crack then finish on DAYTRIPPER DIRECT.

FA Mike Artz, Eddie Begoon

The bolt is scary to clip, but it usually sports a helper sling.

26 DAYTRIPPER 5.10a *

Begin about 20 ft. left of RIGHT TOPE, below a narrow right-facing corner that starts 20 ft. off the ground.

#1 Climb up to the corner. Follow the corner to its end. Traverse up and left toward the buttress and look for cold shuts above SLIPSTREAM (80 ft.)

#2 You can climb easier rock to the top, although most parties do only the first pitch.

FA John Bercaw, J. Garrahan

27 DAYTRIPPER DIRECT 5.11a *

#1 Set up a hanging belay at the end of the right-facing corner of DAYTRIPPER. (60 ft.)

#2 Climb the crack for 10 ft. until you reach a horizontal crack. Traverse right along the horizontal crack to another vertical crack. Climb this crack to a ledge. (100 ft.)

FA unknown

Up the grade if you do it in one long pitch. The protection is good but difficult to place.

Harrison Shull on JUDGMENT SEAT (5.10a). (Photo: Tony Barnes.)

28 DOUBLE D DIRECT 5.11c
(Var.) From the hanging belay at the end of the first pitch of DAYTRIPPER, traverse left to an obvious vertical crack. Climb the thin cracks and face to a stubby evergreen tree and ledge. (50 ft.)
FA Drew Bedford, Ed Begoon, Mike Artz 1986
The protection is good but difficult to place.

29 STOP MAKING SENSE 5.12b
Located just right of SLIPSTREAM.
#1 Climb the face just right of the regular start of SLIPSTREAM. Climb a crack to a horizontal crack. Continue past a bolt to the top of SLIPSTREAM. (70 ft.)
FA Greg Smith, Mike Artz

30 SLIPSTREAM 5.10a *
The start is the same as DAYTRIPPER.
#1 Climb up flakes for 15 ft to a ledge. Traverse left for 10 ft. then climb thin cracks in the face aiming for a left-facing corner/flake. Follow the flake to the belay. (70 ft.)
#2 Finish on easier rock.
FA Howard Doyle, Chris Rowins

31 SLIPSTREAM DIRECT 5.10a
Begin three feet left of the start of DAYTRIPPER.
#1 At a point below the end of the leftward traverse on DAYTRIPPER, climb straight up to a large shelf. Diagonal up and left via jugs, working toward the upper section of SLIPSTREAM.
FA Howard Doyle, Eric Janoscrat
The protection is good but difficult to place.

32 RHODODENDRON CORNER 5.7+
Start at the base of the prominent western buttress.
#1 Climb the awkward face on the right side of the north face of the buttress. Climb right of an overhang via a short crack. Easier climbing leads to ledges.
#2 Make an easy traverse right.
#3 Climb the easy corner to the top. (100 ft.)
FA John Christian, Arnold Wexler
It's possible to combine the 1st and 2nd pitches.

33 GEPHARDT-DUFTY 5.7+
The start is the same as RHODODENDRON CORNER.
#1 Climb the narrow north face of the buttress to a good belay. The first section is the same as the start of RHODODENDRON CORNER (110 ft.)
#2 Continue to the top of the buttress. (115 ft.)
#3 Traverse across the top of the GREAT CHIMNEY to the neighboring buttress. Climb it to the top. (60 ft.)
FA Bob Gephardt, Bob Dufty
This route offers spectacular situations, although on sometimes questionable rock. Route finding is difficult in places. Many variations are possible.

33

32

22   21

30

SOUTHERN PILLAR

33

34 GREAT CHIMNEY 5.1

Begin directly at the base of the large chimney that splits the main Southern Pillar into the GEPHART-DUFTY (west) and INITIATION (east) buttresses.

#1 Climb the chimney to a belay. (150 ft.)

#2 Continue to the top. (115 ft.)

FA Mark Carpenter, Tal Bielefeldt 1965

35 INITIATION 5.4

This route is located on the eastern buttress. Start from a ledge on the buttress, just left of GREAT CHIMNEY.

#1 Climb the narrow north face to a ledge near the top. (135 ft.)

#2 Finish easily up to the top.

FA John Markwell, John Christian 1971

36 MRS. ROBINSON 5.6

Begin on the left side of the prominent INITIATION buttress, below a large detached flake.

#1 Climb straight up the crack aiming for a vegetated ledge. (40 ft.)

#2 Climb the chimney. (100 ft.)

#3 Move up and left to a large block. Climb to the top of the block, then left to a ledge. (100 ft.)

FA Roger Birch, Bob Robinson 1970

37 SOUTHERN THRILLER 5.11b

Hike about fifty yards up the base of the east face of the Southern Pillar. Climb fourth class terrain to the foot of the arete formed by the upper northeast (left) edge of the INITIATION buttress. Alternately, climb INITIATION to this point.

#1 Climb straight up the arete past six bolts to a cold shut anchor (50 ft.)

FA Tom Cecil, Darell Hensley 1993

Routes #38-43 are located even farther up the east side of the Southern Pillar. Hike up the steep slope on the east side of the formation for about 100 yds to a large broken overhang on the wall.

38 A BITTER END 5.9+

About 100 yds past the start of GEPHARDT-DUFTY is a large conifer that lies about 25 ft. from the rocks with branches on the downhill side only. From the tree, walk toward the rock and down about 20 ft. to a smooth face with a crack.

#1 Climb the crack approximately 25 ft. to the tree. Belay 15 ft. left of the tree in the corner.

#2 Climb the crack in the center of the face to the overhang above. Traverse right for about 10 ft. to the end of the overhang. Climb a right-facing corner to a belay. (75 ft.)

FA Howard Doyle, Eric Janoscrat 1980

39 SILENT SCREAM 5.9+
From the large tree mentioned in A BITTER END, continue uphill for about 15 yds to a large orange roof. Approximately 25 ft. below the overhang is a 3" diameter pine on a ledge. Start at the pine.
#1 Climb the face 8 ft. right of the small pine. Climb up and right, aiming for a large right-facing corner that splits the overhang near its right end. Surmount the small roof to gain the corner. Move up to the larger roof, then traverse left 10 ft. to the nose. Climb over the nose and up the face to a tree near the right hand side of the ledge.
FA Howard Doyle, Mike Whitman

40 AWAY FROM THE FLOW 5.9-
Start 8 ft. left of the small pine mentioned in SILENT SCREAM.
#1 Climb up the right-facing flakes and corners directly to the large roof. Climb over the roof to a large left-facing corner/detached pinnacle. Continue up the face, just left of the pinnacle. Move left 8 ft. and continue up the crack system and face to the ledge.
FA Howard Doyle, Mike Whitman

41 INTO THE MYSTIC 5.7
Start at the left edge of the large overhang, just left of AWAY FROM THE FLOW.
#1 Start below the roof, then move up and left. Work through on the left side, then move up to the lichen free area on the wall. Continue to easy ledges.(65 ft.)
FA Harvey Graef, Bob Johnson 1977

42 MYSTICAL MEMBRANE 5.9
Start on the same ledge as INTO THE MYSTIC.
#1 Climb the crack to the left-facing corner. Move onto the right wall and climb this to a tree. (90 ft.)
#2 About 10 ft. right of the tree is an alcove in an orange face. Climb the crack and left-facing corner straight to the tree. (40 ft.)
FA Chris Guenther, Eric Janoscrat, Pannil Jones

43 THE FRAGMATIST 5.7
Begin from the same ledge as MYSTICAL MEMBRANE.
#1 Climb the crack (same as MYSTICAL MEMBRANE) to the left side of the left-facing corner to the ledge. Climb a 5.6 crack to the left of the corner to a large tree. Continue through an overhanging wall to a tree. (115 ft.)
FA Eric Janoscrat, Pannil Jones 1983

THE SOUTH END

The small stream that parallels Roy Gap Road has carved a dramatic gap in East Seneca Ridge, south of the main summits. The Southern Pillar lies on the south side of this gap. The South End, which forms the north side of the gap is truly imposing. The South End is a large overhanging wall consisting of many cracks, corners, and ramps. The face rises steeply above the short talus slope, almost directly above the stream. Many of Seneca's most breath-taking routes ascend this wall. Despite the steep nature of the wall, several excellent moderate routes can be found here. From left to right, major features of the South End are: the Ecstasy Buttress, MUSCLE BEACH area, The Cave, the Totem Buttress, and the Skyline Buttress.

Please note that it is very difficult to retreat from the upper portions of routes that lie above the Cave, especially if you are climbing with a single rope.

APPROACH

Most South End and all Southwest Corner routes are approached by the West Face Trail which is marked with blue blazes. The trail begins below a huge old oak which has fallen across Roy Gap Run to form a slippery natural bridge (an option when the stream is too high). The normal trail fords the run left of the log. Hike thirty yards up the hill, just left of the standing trunk. A feeder trail on the right cuts directly east to the Southwest Corner and the base of ECSTASY. All other South End routes can be approached by following the trail along the base of the South End. The trail, which is marked with blue blazes, avoids the steep, delicate screes and soils.

Approach the climbs on the far right side of the South End by continuing on Roy Gap Road until about fifty feet past the culvert pipe. On your left find a post with a blue blaze. The trail climbs the talus a short distance before turning left near the toe of the Skyline Buttress. Follow switchbacks up to the CANDY CORNER/TOTEM area.

PLEASE DO NOT forge your own way up through the fragile vegetation and talus directly below the South End.

44 ECSTASY 5.7 *
Begin below the sloping buttress at the extreme left side of the South End.
#1   Climb twenty-five feet through an easy chimney to a large ledge at the base of a white face with vertical cracks. Climb the face to a ledge beneath an overhang. (100 ft.) This pitch can be broken into 2 shorter pitches by belaying on the large ledge 25 ft. up the buttress.
#2   Move right into a wide crack. Climb up about 15 ft. and then start traversing right and up across the wildly exposed face. Pass a projecting pedestal of lichened quartzite and climb right-leaning cracks to a small stance with several old fixed pitons. (70 ft.)
#3   Make an easy 8 ft. traverse right from the belay to the base of a steep crack. Climb up and over a bulge, and weave your way up until you can top out to the left of a pine which overhangs the face. (55 ft.)
FA   Joe Faint & party.
This route is continuous and exposed, always exciting but never outrageous: a classic.

The South End as seen from the Southern Pillar.

45 SOUTHWEST BUTTRESS VARIATION 5.5
(Var.) Climb the first pitch of ECSTASY. Begin the second pitch, but at the point ECSTASY traverses right, continue straight up the wide crack to a large ledge. Finish on ECSTASY JUNIOR or rappel from the tree with the overhanging crook (100 ft. to the ground!).

46 VALLEY VIEW 5.9 **R**
Start in the large right-facing dihedral formed by the lower ECSTASY buttress. This corner is 10 ft. left of SOUTHERN EXPOSURE and 25 ft. left of SIXTH SENSE.
#1 Climb the right side of the large dihedral, five feet right of the actual corner. Move through a small overhang with a prominent crack. This crack forms a right-facing corner. Continue to the top of the cracks. Diagonal up and left across the face, aiming for a shallow left-facing corner. Climb the corner, then diagonal up and left to a belay on ECSTASY. (140 ft.)
#2 Climb up and right to a small ledge. Climb up and left across the face. Follow discontinuous cracks to a small overhang. Move up and right, then back left, aiming for a small bush. Go straight up to the top. (60 ft.)
FA Mike Perliss, Ed McCarthy

47 SOUTHERN EXPOSURE 5.9
About 20 ft. left of the start of SIXTH SENSE are several small trees. Start at the trees.
#1 Climb the broken face to a right-facing corner. Climb the corner. After about 40 ft. the corner turns into a right-leaning ramp. This ramp leads to SIXTH SENSE. Instead of climbing the ramp, move left until it is possible to climb the left side of a small outside corner. Climb up past a small tree to the ECSTASY belay. (150 ft.)
#2 Finish on ECSTASY.
FA Howard Doyle, Eric Janoscrat 1978
The protection is reasonable. Take many small to medium nuts and plenty of slings.

48 SIXTH SENSE 5.10a
Approximately 25 ft. from the left side of the unmistakable Cave there is a small black sloping ramp in a right-facing corner leading to several overhangs.
#1 Climb the ramp, then step left around the overhangs. Climb up to a good hanging belay with cold shuts. (50 ft.)
#2 Continue up and left passing several small overhangs. Climb past the traverse of ECSTASY and establish a belay at the base of the large right-facing corner at the top of the cliff.
#3 Climb the corner and the final overhang to the top. (50 ft.)
FA Bob Williams, Barry Wallen 1966
FFA Matt Hale, Ray Snead 1973

49 MUSCLE BEACH 5.11b *
Between the start of SIXTH SENSE and the left side of the large cave are several trees below a large square cut roof.
#1 Scramble up and left, aiming for a corner and crack on the left side of the large roof. Take the roof on the left and continue for about 15 ft. to a hanging belay at rappel hangers. (50 ft.)

Harrison Shull on SPINNAKER (5.10c).   (Photo: Darell Hensley.)

#2   Climb up and right to a niche. Continue up and over a bulge to a set of twin cracks. Climb the cracks until they end. Step left at the top of the cracks and climb steep rock to a rappel hanger belay at the far left side of the SIMPLE J. MALARKEY ledge. (90 ft.)

#3   Climb the white corner for about 5 ft. Step right, then continue straight through the roof. (40 ft.)

FA   Ray Snead, Matt Hale 1975

Take a trip to the BEACH this weekend, but don't get sand kicked in your face.

50   DRACULA 5.12a *

#1   Climb easy rock on the right side of a 20 foot tower, just left of the Cave's mouth. Move left beneath the small roof. Move up and over the small roof, past 3 bolts. Traverse slightly left to MUSCLE BEACH to finish, or continue straight up past five or six more bolts (110 ft.).

FA   Tom Cecil, Steve Cater 1989 (DRACULA BEACH, 5.11c)

FA   Dir. Finish Porter Jarrard 1991

This route needed an anchor as of this writing.

51   SUPERSTITION 5.11c R

Start at the left edge of the Cave, at the same point as for DRACULA.

#1   Climb broken ledges 15 ft. to a large right-facing corner. Move up the corner for about 15-20 ft. until you reach the overhangs. Move left, then up through the large overhang to a hanging belay below the next roof. (60 ft.)

#2   Turn the next overhang by moving left. Continue up a crack until it is possible to move right to a large right-facing open book. Climb the book to a corner. Climb the corner past a small tree to the SIMPLE J. MALARKEY ramp. (70 ft.)

#3   Finish on SIMPLE J. MALARKEY.

FA   Thayer Hughes, Mike Perraglio

FFA Eric Janoscrat, Howard Doyle 1978

This sustained route was free climbed on Friday the 13th. Beware of bad rock on the second pitch. The route requires a large rack. Four leaf clovers and rabbits feet are optional.

52   SUPERSTITION DIRECT START 5.11d

(Var.) From the broken ledges at the start of the regular route, go up the left-facing corner, directly beneath the flared crack in the roof. Move through the roof and link up with the rest of SUPERSTITION.

FA   Marty McLaughlin 1982

53   THE THREAT 5.12b *

Begin just inside the Cave's mouth, right of the previously mentioned tower.

#1   Climb easy rock to a short flake and clip a bolt. Move up and slightly right on a steep, textured, orange face past more bolts to a strenuous bulge with cracks on either side. Crank over this and climb on polished holds to a bolt anchor in an alcove. There are seven bolts in all. (60 ft.)

FA   Tom Cecil, Eric Anderson, Brian McCray 1992

ECSTASY BUTTRESS

SOUTH END - ECSTASY BUTTRESS AND CAVE AREA

THE CAVE

57

65

68

TOTEM BUTTRESS 75 SKYLINE BUTTRESS

SOUTH END—TOTEM & SKYLINE BUTTRESSES

Harrison Shull on THE THREAT (5.12b).   (Photo: Darell Hensley.)

54 FINE YOUNG CANNIBALS 5.12d/13a *
Begin inside the Cave, on the left (west) wall.
#1 Climb a shallow corner and a crack which is studded with old pitons, past three bolts. Clip the cold shut anchor but continue up and left, out and over the lip of the cave. Belay over the lip.
FFA John Bercaw, Rod Hansen 1988
This is the old SATISFACTION #1 aid route. The pitch was freed to the point of the cold shuts by Cal Swoager in 1981, creating Seneca's first 5.12 pitch (5.12c). An anchor nest of old slings and pitons at the top of this section was clipped as protection during the first ascent of CANNIBALS. In 1992 it was replaced by cold shuts, and the three bolts were added.

55 CAVEMEN 5.10d
Start near the back of the cave.
#1 Climb out the crack on the left side to the old 1/4" bolt belay.
FA Mark Carpenter, Barry Wallen
FFA Cal Swoager, Eric Janoscrat 1981
This is the old SATISFACTION #2 aid route. Look out for bats in the hand and finger locks.

56 NIGHTMARE (project)
Start in the back right recess of the cave. A desperate line of upside-down climbing heads toward the lip of the Cave past several bolts. The route had not been redpointed at the time of this writing, and its creator Brian McCray was contemplating relocating the clips nearest the lip.

57 SIMPLE J. MALARKEY 5.7 *
Start outside the right (east) side of the Cave entrance, just beyond a large ledge.
#1 Pick your way up the steep, black face directly below a large rubble-covered alcove with a good-sized tree. TCU's or similar protection make this a safer pitch. (35 ft.)
#2 Ascend the obvious low-angle ramp which shoots up and left out of the alcove. The ramp is broken at one place. Continue past the break to the apparent end of the ramp. (75 ft.)
#3 Climb up the steep wall, angling right to easier ground. (60 ft.)
FA Jim McCarthy, Arnold Wexler 1954
FFA unknown
This is an interesting route through an overhanging wall, made possible by the large ramp that splits the wall. Try one of the variations to finish. The best finish is perhaps the last pitch of MUSCLE BEACH (5.8). A hair-raising incident occurred in 1991 in which riled ground hornets stung a climber in the rubble-covered alcove. The stung climber knocked rocks toward her belayer and cut the rope. Fortunately, no one was seriously hurt. This was only one of many known epics that seem to dog parties on this route. Most of the excitement seems to take place on the third pitch.

58   SJM CAVE START 5.8 R

(Var.) At the right (east) side of the cave entrance is a smooth dihedral leading to overlapping roofs. This is only one of various ways to begin SJM from inside the Cave.

#1   Climb the dihedral past poor protection (or climb anywhere along the Cave wall farther left) and up the ramp to a point below the roof (good gear here). Clip nasty pitons over the lip and pull the roof. Work out right and up into the large rubble covered alcove. (45 ft.)

#2   Continue on SJM.

The fixed anchor before the exit moves allows a rainy day toprope, although at the time of this writing the bolts were in somewhat questionable blocks.

FA   Unknown

59   SJM WESTERLY EXTENSION

(Var.) At the end of the regular second pitch it is possible to move left around the corner another 15 ft. to an exposed ledge at a right-facing corner. All the variations to the last pitch start here.

60   SJM TRAVERSE FINISH 5.6

(Var.) From the belay, climb straight up the corner about 10 ft until it is possible to traverse out right. Climb right, around the corner, to easier ground. Move up to the top. (70 ft.)

61   SJM OVERHANG FINISH 5.8 *

(Var.) This is also the last pitch of MUSCLE BEACH. Climb up the steep corner until below the obvious overhang. Pull the overhang at its widest point. (40 ft.)

62   SJM ECSTASY CONNECTION 5.6

(Var.) It is possible to downclimb from the ledge and move left around a corner to the belay on ECSTASY. Finish by climbing the last pitch of ECSTASY.

63   WELCOME TO SENECA 5.10d

The start is the same as SIMPLE J. MALARKEY.

#1   Climb the first pitch of SIMPLE J. MALARKEY.

#2   From the tree, climb the ramp to the right. Follow the ramp for 25 ft. to a white face. Climb the right-facing corner of the large flake, then move left. Continue straight up to the base of the flared chimney. Climb through the chimney and overhang to a small ledge. (75 ft.)

#3   Climb the remainder of the buttress, keeping to the left side. (100 ft.)

FA   George Livingstone, Thais Weibel 1967

FFA Howard Doyle, Marty McLaughlin, Eric Janoscrat 1978

This strenuous route requires a large rack. There are areas of loose rock.

64   WILD MEN ONLY 5.11b

To the right of the Cave and SJM is the prominent sloping Totem buttress, which rises to meet a large roof.

#1   Climb the left side of the buttress to a belay beneath the left side of the huge roof. (90 ft.)

#2   Pull the overhang at its widest point then continue up a squeeze chimney. After the chimney continue to the base of an overhang. Traverse left, then move up to a ledge. (145 ft.)

#3   Stay to the right of the overhangs and continue up the buttress to the top. (80 ft.)

FA Tom Evans, Chips Janger, Bob Lyon 1967

FFA John Bercaw, John Gorrahan 1976

Wild women are also welcome.

65 TOTEM 5.11a *

Begin right of WILD MEN ONLY.

#1   Climb the Totem Buttress to a belay at cold shuts beneath the right side of the roof. (85 ft.)

#2   Follow the line of fixed pins out and over the roof. Belay at a small stance. Cold shuts (25 ft.)

#3   Follow the obvious inside corner up the buttress, through an overhang to a short wall. Climb the wall and move up to a stance. (125 ft.)

#4   Climb the corner to the top of the wall.(50 ft.)

FA Ivan Jirak

FFA John Stannard 1971

66 SCROTUM 5.10a R/X

(Var.) Traverse about 10 ft. to the right of the roof pitch. Climb the overhang at this point. (45 ft.)

This unprotected pitch takes balls to lead.

67 BLOOD ON THE TRACKS 5.10b R

Begin directly beneath the right side (east face) of the Totem Buttress, about 20 ft. left of TONY'S NIGHTMARE.

#1   Climb the thin cracks in the center of the wall. Aficionados will claim the left edge of the buttress is off route. (70 ft.)

FA Leith Wain, Mark Huth

68 TONY'S NIGHTMARE 5.6

Start just to the right of the Totem Buttress below an obvious "A" shaped chimney. The route starts on the ramp below the chimney.

#1   Climb the ramp and corner up to a sloping ledge at the base of a short wall. Climb the wall and set up a belay beneath an overhang formed by a large chockstone. (70 ft.)

#2   Climb past the chockstone into the large chimney. Start up the chimney until it is possible to exit right to a good ledge. (50 ft.)

#3   Finish on SKYLINE TRAVERSE.

FA Tony Soler, Ray Moore, Lorraine Snyder 1950

The chimney is a favorite hangout for pigeons. The white stuff is not chalk.

69   TONY'S NIGHTMARE DIRECT FINISH 5.7
(Var.) On the last pitch, climb straight out the chimney and up the corner above. (95 ft.)

70   EASY SKANKIN' 5.9-
#1   On the face just left of TONY'S NIGHTMARE DIRECT FINISH, climb past five bolts to a bolt anchor. (50 ft.)
FA   Darell Hensley and Ashton Walton 1993

71   QUARTZ INVERSION 5.9 *
Start high on the cliff, left of and slightly below the start of EASY SKANKIN'.
#1   Climb discontinuous cracks in the wall to a tree at the top. (75 ft.)
This climb is a good alternative finish for NIGHTWINGS.

72   PYTHON 5.9 R
Start above and to the right of the second pitch of SKYLINE TRAVERSE and about 30 ft. right of TONY'S NIGHTMARE DIRECT FINISH.
#1   Climb the overhanging rock rib inside the east wall of the Skyline Chimney. Exit right about 4 ft. from the top.
FA   Paul Anikis, Howard Doyle

73   THE DAYDREAM 5.9+ R
Just to the left of the YE GODS corner, there is an obvious rectangular cave. Start near the left side of the cave.
#1   Climb the steep, grungy, loose and dangerous wall to a belay at the base of the large overhangs. (70 ft.)
FA   Howard Doyle, Lotus Steele 1975

74   NIGHTWINGS 5.10b
Climb THE DAYDREAM or TONY'S NIGHTMARE to the ledges at the base of the large overhangs to the left of YE GODS.
#1   Climb up the left-facing corner near the left side of the roof. Continue up over-hanging corners to a small pedestal beneath the main roof. Climb through the roof, then step up to a belay. Strenuous and loose (85 ft.)
FA   Chick Holtkamp, Carol Black 1978

75   YE GODS AND LITTLE FISHES 5.8 *
The large buttress on the right side of the South End (Skyline Buttress) forms a huge left-facing corner. Start at the ramp at the bottom of the corner and right of the rectangular cave.
#1   Climb the steep corner straight up to a large ledge. Locate cold shuts to the right. (85 ft.)
#2   Use the orange and black flake on the left wall in the back of the wide chimney to surmount the overhang. Finish on the second pitch of SKYLINE TRAVERSE. (60 ft.)
#3   Finish on SKYLINE TRAVERSE.
FA   Arnold Wexler, John Reed, Earl Mosburg 1953
FFA unknown

76 DROP ZONE 5.11b *
Begin to the right of YE GODS, on the right wall of the huge open book (west face of the Skyline Buttress).
#1 Climb horizontal and vertical cracks straight up the smooth, steep wall. There is one fixed pin. Cold shuts (shared by YE GODS and CANDY CORNER). (85 ft.)
FA Marty McLaughlin, Howard Doyle, Eric Janoscrat 1978

77 CANDY CORNER 5.5 *
Start at the base of the narrow left-leaning dihedral fifteen feet right of DROP ZONE.
#1 Climb the corner to its top. Belay at cold shuts on the ledge above DROP ZONE or continue up and right to the SKYLINE TRAVERSE belay. (95 ft.)
#2 Finish on SKYLINE TRAVERSE.
FA unknown

78 LSD (LOWER SKYLINE DIRECT) 5.5
Begin around the corner right of the start of CANDY CORNER, in a gully on the broken lower section of the Skyline Buttress.
#1 Climb up the broken section until the climbing starts to get a little harder. (30 ft.)
#2 Climb the chimney above up to the SKYLINE TRAVERSE belay ledge. It is difficult to protect a twenty foot section of wide crack climbing. (90 ft.)
FA Paul Bradt, Don Hubbard, Sam Moore 1939

79 SKYLAB 5.9
(Var.) This route is believed to lie on the east face of the Lower Skyline Buttress. Climb a crack in the center of the face to rejoin LSD.
FA Greg Collins, Paul Billups

80 LA BELLA VISTA 5.10a *
This route starts at about the same level as the top of the first pitch of LSD. It follows the edge of the fin formed by the merging of the Skyline Buttress and the East Face.
#1 Climb the right edge of the very narrow buttress, past an overhang, to the SKYLINE TRAVERSE belay ledge.
#2 From the old ring belay bolts of SKYLINE TRAVERSE, climb up the steep arete, passing the final overhang on its left side. (85 ft.)
FA Howard Doyle, Lotus Steele

81 LOTUS VARIATION
(Var.) At the overhang on the first pitch, move right to a crack. Follow the crack to the top of the first pitch.

82 BIRDS OF PREY 5.10b **R**
#1 From the tree belay at the end of the second pitch of SKYLINE TRAVERSE (inside the huge SKYLINE chimney) climb the west face of the LA BELLA VISTA fin, following a thin rounded flake. This route is located to the right of PYTHON (#72).
FA Paul Anikis, Mark Thesing 1984

Nannet Seligman on CANDY CORNER (5.5). (Photo: Darell Hensley.)

83 SPINNAKER 5.10c *
Start on the steep ramp in the chimney midway up the second pitch of SKYLINE TRAVERSE.
#1   Climb the outrageous west face and arete of the LA BELLA VISTA fin, right of BIRDS OF PREY. There are eight bolts, and a cold shut anchor at the top of the rib. (65 ft.)
FA Darell Hensley, Chris Leon 1992

84 THE SHAMBLER 5.8
The start is the same as ECSTASY.
#1-3   Climb ECSTASY through its second pitch. Climb SJM ECSTASY CON-NECTION.
#4   Traverse up and right, aiming for the bottomless black gully and a belay. (50 ft.)
#5   Cross the gully and move across the Totem Buttress. Climb down to the TONY'S NIGHTMARE belay. (60 ft.)
#6   Finish on TONY'S NIGHTMARE and SKYLINE TRAVERSE.
FA Ray Snead, Ben Mealy 1974

This route is more than a girdle traverse, it's a circumnavigation of the entire Seneca Rocks formation. The route was established over a period of two years via rope solo. The final push was a fourteen hour, forty pitch, 3,000 foot effort.

SENECA TRAIL 5.8

P.1-2	Climb the first two pitches of ECSTASY (5.7).
P.3	Climb the SJM-ECSTASY CONNECTION, to the black gully (5.6).
P.4	Cross the gully above the pine and mount the Totem Buttress on the Southwest corner (5.1).
P.5	Cross the Totem Buttress on the obvious breakdown (5.1).
P.6	Traverse the finger lip/crack into TONY'S NIGHTMARE, then move down toward the tree. Look for a baby angle pin. (SHAMBLER crux) Scramble up to the SKYLINE TRAVERSE belay tree (5.8).
P.7	Down climb the 2nd pitch of SKYLINE TRAVERSE (5.3).
P.8	Lead out on the east face on DUFTY'S, jump off on KAUFFMAN-CARDON, belay at the obvious tree (5.5).
P.9	Follow KAUFFMAN-CARDON to Broadway Ledge (5.3).
P.10	Up A CHRISTIAN DELIGHT to OLD LADIES (5.3).
P.11	Climb OLD LADIES 2nd pitch to its end (5.0).
P.12-13	Follow AMAZING GRACE to its end on Soler Flake (5.7).
P.14	Cross to CONN'S EAST to the end of the 2nd pitch (5.5).
P.15	Two options. Finish CONN'S EAST or from halfway up CONN'S EAST traverse directly across the HIGH TEST area to above the Gryphon's Beak (5.8, the crux).
P.16	Downclimb GUNSIGHT TO SOUTH PEAK (5.3).
P.17	Cross northeast to the base of GUNSIGHT TO NORTH PEAK (5.0).
P.18	Downclimb obvious steps, turn north to the small pine halfway up LICHEN OR LEAVE IT (5.2).
P.19	Climb LICHEN OR LEAVE IT (5.8).
P.20	Traverse north to the ROUX 1st pitch belay tree (5.0).
P.21	Traverse up and down and north to the ROX SALT 1st pitch belay stance (5.2).
P.22	Traverse up and north to the large tree atop the SALLY'S PERIL flake pitch (5.3).
P.23	Follow easy ledge systems up, down and north to the very base of HEFFALUMP TRAP (5.1). Don't touch down!

P.24　　Climb HEFFALUMP TRAP. Stand on North Summit (5.3).

P.25　　Very carefully scramble down to the top of No Dally Alley. Step cross, move south 20 feet, and down climb the obvious ramp to the dark alley bottom (5.5).

P.26　　Walk through No Dally Alley to the south entrance.

P.27　　Climb WEST FACE TO GUNSIGHT until below the BELL.

P.28　　Under the BELL, move down ledges until atop NOVA.

P.29　　Move directly south to GREENWALL, pitch 2.

P.30　　New pitch. Climb up and south across the white face to the PLEASANT OVERHANGS hanging belay (5.5).

P.31　　Down climb PLEASANT OVERHANGS pitch 2 (5.7).

P.32　　Down climb THAIS DIRECT pitch 2 (5.6).

P.33　　Follow ledges west then south to WEST POLE.

P.34-35　Climb OLD MAN'S ROUTE to the TRAFFIC JAM rappel tree.

P.36-37　Reverse HORRENDOUS TRAVERSE into Windy Notch (5.7).

P.38-39　Reverse COCKSCOMB PINE TREE, OLD LADIES traverse. From Luncheon Ledge scramble south to the top of the Southern End, above ECSTASY JUNIOR.

P.40　　Rappel to the ECSTASY JUNIOR/BURN wall area.

F.A. Mike Carroll, 1993/94 F.A. Continuous, Mike Carroll/Larry Singleton, 1994

SOUTH PEAK-WEST FACE

This face has Seneca's greatest concentration of popular routes. The South Peak-West Face sports many classic routes of all grades. The face is easily viewed from the town of Seneca Rocks. The right side of the face starts as a wedge of rock rising from the vicinity of Roy Gap Road. This area, the Southwest Corner, is located below and primarily to the right of the main cliff.

Above the Southwest Corner is the main West Face of the South Peak. Starting on the right skyline, the first prominent pinnacle is Humphrey's Head. Next is the larger Cockscomb with its curved summit. The left side of the Cockscomb joins with the Face of a Thousand Pitons to form a huge dihedral. The south-facing Face of a Thousand Pitons is not visible from the road. From here the rocks rise to the true South Peak summit which can only be reached by 5th class climbing. The left side of the South Peak is a sweeping drop that ends in the Gunsight Notch.

APPROACH

A good trail system provides easy access to every route on the face. Cross Roy Gap Run just west of the Southwest Corner. The blue marked trail is fairly obvious on the far side of the stream. A massive oak tree on the far side fell across the stream in 1991 and is a possible foot bridge when the water levels are high. Follow the trail up steep rocky terrain to the left of the stump of the great oak. Continue to the south edge of a rock fin standing separate from the main Southwest Corner. This is the Block, which has some good top-roping. The South End and Southwest Corner are reached by following the feeder trail to the right (east). The trail is encountered just below the Block (this short trail continues across the base of the South End and back down to Roy Gap Road).

The upper South Peak is reached by staying on the main trail. Please remember to use all of the switchbacks. After 100 yards or so the trail levels out in a small grove of hemlock trees. After the hemlock grove, hike up a talus slope to two short 3rd class steps (which may be treacherous when wet or icy). The trail forks in the upper talus, with branches ending just to the right of the base of the Cockscomb (Luncheon Ledge) and at the base of Le Gourmet. Luncheon Ledge, just below Humphrey's Head, is a popular meeting spot, hang out, and lunch area. The start of OLD LADIES ROUTE (5.2) is here. To reach the rest of the South Peak-West Face follow the trail north along the base.

Please try to follow marked trails and avoid loose soil on the third class terrain. The trails were built by other climbers, usually in the rain, in order to slow the erosion on the hillside. You might also consider spending a few days on trail duty yourself.

REFLECTORS ARE USED TO MARK THE TRAIL FOR THE RESCUE LITTER. DO NOT WALK ON THIS TRAIL.

DESCENT

It is necessary to either rappel or downclimb 5th class terrain to descend from the upper South Peak. Rappel routes go down both East and West Faces. East Face rappel routes go to Broadway Ledge. See the DESCENT description for the South Peak-

East Face for a description of these routes.

In order to descend to the base of the West Face, use the standard rappel routes that start at the top of OLD MAN'S ROUTE, at the west entrance of the chimney located on the far south end of the summit ledge (Traffic Jam Chimney). Rappel ropes of 165 ft. or longer are recommended. For both descent routes, begin at the pine tree at the top of the last pitch of OLD MAN'S.

The OLD MAN'S-NECK PRESS rappel goes from a pair of rappel hangers (1/2" bolts) straight down the west face to the narrow south end of the Old Man's Traverse Ledge where there are more drilled anchors (45 ft.) From here two ropes reach the ground down the NECK PRESS dihedrals area. If you only have one rope stop at the cold shuts 65 ft. below at the top of the first pitch of NECK PRESS. These are 70 ft. above the ground.

The OLD MAN'S-FRONT C rappel route goes down and tends left (north) over the widest part of the Old Man's Traverse Ledge to a large pine with slings and rings (55 ft.) With two 165 ft. ropes it's possible to reach the ground from this tree. This ledge atop the FRONT C face is also marked by the stump of a birch tree that died from repeated rappels.

If you have only one rope, rappel from the pine to reach the LE GOURMET TRAVERSE LEDGE (50 ft). Move north about 20 ft. to the last tree, which has a piton actually hammered into the wood. This old oddity is not an anchor! Rappel from the chain or directly off the base of the tree. If a 150 ft. rope is used, the rappel will place the climber on a sloping ledge about 10 ft. off the ground. Scramble down to the trail.

An alternative descent route to the base of the West Face is the CONN'S WEST rappel. Start from the tree at the end of THAIS ESCAPE and CONN'S WEST DIRECT, about 200 ft north of the OLD MAN'S rappel routes via the summit ledge. This starts at a pine with slings and rings on a ledge ten feet (5.0) below the south end of the actual summit ridge. From here two ropes (140 ft.) take you to the ledge and rappel tree at the base of WEST POLE, 70 ft. above the ground.

If you have only one rope, rappel from the first pine (atop CONN'S WEST DIRECT and THAIS ESCAPE) to a rubble covered ledge with a good-sized birch with slings and rings (50 ft). This tree is at the base of the large, chockstoned CONN'S WEST chimney. From here rappel 65 ft. and traverse left (north) to the tree previously mentioned, at the base of WEST POLE.

Some experienced climbers downclimb OLD LADIES' and OLD MAN'S. However, a slip from most positions on these routes would most likely result in the death of the climber (as occurred in the case of an unroped climber in 1994). In addition, on crowded weekends the routes are used continuously.

Several areas on the South Peak deserve special mention.

Humphrey's Head is generally descended by climbing down via the north ridge or rappelling the west face. The best descent for The Cockscomb is to downclimb the north ridge into Windy Notch (above TRIPLE S), climb the last pitch of WINDY CORNER (5.4), then use either the East Face or West Face rappel routes.

The west side of the Gunsight can be descended on rappel from the straight white pine on a smooth sloping ledge just below the Gunsight (85 ft.) Another option is to walk north and downslope about thirty yards to a pine with an extreme crook in its trunk. This rappel is about 35 ft.

All West Face routes read from right to left. The first South End route around the corner to the right of THE BURN is ECSTASY.

85 THE BURN 5.8 *
About halfway between the right edge of the Southwest Corner and a vegetated ramp there is a narrow right-facing corner/flake. Start below and right of the corner, up on a block with a small tree.
#1   Climb the corner and cracks in the face to the ledge beneath an overhang. Climb through the overhang, stepping left to a small stance. Climb the finger cracks straight up to the huge ECSTASY JUNIOR belay ledge. (100 ft.)
#2   Climb the center of the face to the right of the large corner. (50 ft.)
FA Jeff Burns, Rich Pleiss 1974
The upper part of the first pitch has beautiful cracks on steep, clean rock. The second pitch is seldom done.

86 BURN ESCAPE
(Var.) The crux of THE BURN can be avoided by stepping left into a small right-facing corner with a tiny pine.

87 ALGAL FRIENDS AND FUNGUS 5.9 R
(Var.) Above the overhang on THE BURN, move right via the ramp and crack system to the southwest outside corner. Climb the outside corner to the large ledge.
FA Roman Dial, Mark Munn 1980
Lots of lichen and not much protection. Bring a #3 Friend.

88 SUNSHINE 5.10a *
Begin just left of THE BURN, beneath a bolt which is about 45 ft. up.
#1   Climb the thin face and cracks to a bolt. If you miss any of the microwire placements down low this pitch will take on at least an "R" protection rating. Climb past the bolt to an overlap, then up a clean white face and finger crack to the ECSTASY JUNIOR ledge. (95 ft.)
FA Jessie Guthrie, Joey Murray 1975

89 MOONSHINE 5.11d R/X (TR)
(Var.) Climb the face just left of SUNSHINE. Join the regular route just below the bolt.
FA Mike Cote, Mike Artz 1986
Bring a #4 TCU and very small nuts.

Chris Tolen on THE BURN (5.8). (Photo: Tony Barnes.)

90 ECSTASY JUNIOR 5.4 *
Just left of the blank-looking MOONSHINE, climb a blocky vegetated ramp to a
ledge with a pine tree. Or, go upslope thirty feet and scramble up and right to the
same ledge.
#1 From the tree move up and right to a balancy foot traverse right. After ten feet or
so follow an obvious vertical crack through a bulge and up to the large tree covered
ledge. (70 ft.)
#2 Climb the large right-facing corner to a small overhang. Climb past the over-
hang and the small cave to a steep face. Climb the crack and face to the top. (80 ft.)
FA Chris Scoredos, Don Jacobs, Roy Britton
A interesting route of moderate nature. Steep but reasonable.

SOUTHWEST CORNER

96

90

THE BLOCK

85

ECSTASY BUTTRESS

91   VEGETABLE VARIATION 5.4
(Var.) From the top of the first pitch move left to a vegetated crack. Climb the crack to the top. (100 ft.)

92   TRAVERSE PITCH 5.5
(Var.) From the first pitch of ECSTASY move left then up to the big ledge of ECSTASY JUNIOR. (40 ft.)

93   LICHEN NEVER SLEEPS 5.9
Use the same start as ECSTASY JUNIOR.
#1   From the large pine tree traverse straight right until just short of the large crack. There is a small roof overhead, after short right-facing corners. Climb straight up to the difficult looking crack that comes out of the roof. Climb up to the ledge.(60 ft.)
#2   About 25 ft. right of the VEGETABLE VARIATION right-facing corner, climb straight up the wall using a left-facing flake. Merge with ROOF TRAVERSE. (80 ft.)
FA   Eric Janoscrat, Barbara Bates, Rick Fairtrace

94   ROOF TRAVERSE 5.7
The start is the same as ECSTASY JUNIOR.
#1   Climb up and right on ECSTASY JUNIOR for about 10 ft. to a steep right-facing corner. Climb the corner, then step left to an easy vegetated crack. Follow this crack to the tree that lies next to the large roof. (The continuation of the crack is VEGETABLE VARIATION). Traverse out right beneath the roof. When the overhang becomes double-tiered pull the roof to a right-facing corner. Follow the corner to the top. (60 ft.)
FA   unknown

95   GERT'S GRUNGY GULLY 5.0
Start just left of ECSTASY JUNIOR.
#1   Climb up and left through the obvious gully. (150 ft.)
FA   Gert Christie

96   MR. NO WRENCH 5.11d
Go up GERT'S GRUNGY GULLY to a good ledge below the large roof of ROOF TRAVERSE. This route is left of the second pitch of ECSTASY JUNIOR.
#1   Follow the smooth face past bolts up to the roof. Crank over the roof and up the face above to a two-bolt anchor.
FA: Ed Begoon, George Powell, Tom Cecil 1993
Note: Carry a few medium-sized nuts.

97   Unnamed 5.10 R/X
Start on the same ledge as the preceding climb.
#1   Climb the face right of MR. NO WRENCH to intersect ROOF TRAVERSE at its right end. Finish on ROOF TRAVERSE.
FA: Ed Begoon, Ben Bullington 1987

98 THE CON MAN 5.9
Begin just left of the VEGETABLE VARIATION and right of GERT'S GRUNGY GULLY at the obvious wall below the DIRTY HAIRY variation.
#1   Climb the short, but obvious, left-facing corner to a ledge (or climb the first pitch of GERT'S GRUNGY GULLY).(50 ft.)
#2   Begin at a short right-facing corner with a tree. Climb straight up the wall, through a roof and up the face above. Climb through a second roof with a cleft. Continue through a third roof. (125 ft.)
FA Howard Doyle, Eric Janoscrat, Paul Anikis

99 WIFE'S A BITCH 5.9+ R
Begin about 15 ft. left of THE CON MAN.
#1   Climb the first pitch of GGG.
#2   Climb the right-facing corner 25 ft. to an overhang. Pull the overhang. Continue up another right-facing corner to the top. (75 ft.)
FA Ed McCarthy, Paul Gillispie, Kenny Hummel
The protection is very sparse above the roof.

100 DIRTY HAIRY 5.6 R
Climb the first 75 ft. of GERT'S GRUNGY GULLY to a good ledge. Climb a right-facing flake to the roof. Step left and over the overhang. Run it out to the top.
FA Mike Whitman, Lori Larson 1980
The pro is good to the roof, but there is nothing above.

Routes #101-104 begin on a rock mass that caps the Southwest Corner. These routes can be gained by first climbing ECSTASY JUNIOR and scrambling/hiking north about 75 yds, then down and back south along the base. However, the easiest approach is via the Hemlock Grove, 3/4 of the way up the West Face Trail. Walk right a short distance—the first route reached is ORGANICALLY INCLINED (#104).

101 BOTTOM TORQUE 5.9+
Begin at the south end of the overhangs capping the Southwest Corner, at an area of low angle slabs. Begin about two feet left of a rusty old piton that lies hidden in an overlap about 6 ft. off the ledge.
#1   Follow the crack straight up through the overhang. Traverse left and up to an opening in an overhang. Climb the overhang and crack, then move up and over a third overhang. Belay at the pine tree. (75 ft.)
FA Mitchell Wood, John Ross 1981

102 THE HANG 5.7
To the left of BOTTOM TORQUE near the middle of the line of overhangs, are two arches. Start near the center of the right arch.
#1   Start on the crack that leads up to the double overhang. Pull both overhangs, then over a third. Belay at a large pine tree.
FA Mitchell Wood 1981

103 FLYING CIRCUS 5.9
Use the same start as THE HANG.
#1 Climb the two lowest overhangs. Follow the shallow left hand crack to the face above. Continue straight up to the large tree that grows next to the boulder. (75 ft.)
Mitchell Wood, John Campbell, Sean Maisel 1981

104 ORGANICALLY INCLINED 5.9
Near the extreme north end of the Southwest Corner, about 30 ft. south of the Hemlock Grove is a relatively large, right-facing corner. Start at a thin crack about 5 ft. left of the corner.
#1 Climb the crack to its top. Step right then continue up crack and face to the top.
FA unknown
FFA Pete Absolon, Topper Wilson 1983

The remainder of the South Peak-West Face routes lie on the main rock mass above and mostly north of the Southwest Corner.

105 HUMPHREY'S HEAD 5.2-5.4 *
The most southerly of the major pinnacles on the right skyline is Humphrey's Head. Many easy routes ascend this small summit. Countless beginners have had their first rock climbing experience on this little pinnacle. Luncheon Ledge is located at the base of Humphrey's Head's west face. A 5.0 downclimb is the usual descent down the north ridge for more experienced climbers. Beginners should descend via top rope or by rappel. (40 ft.)

106 OLD LADIES' ROUTE 5.2 *
Begin on the Luncheon Ledge, at the gap between Humphrey's Head and the Cockscomb.
#1 Climb up through the notch between Humphrey's Head and the Cockscomb. Belay on a flat ledge with a view to the east. (100 ft.)
#2 Move out onto the East Face by moving right and then down. After one exciting move, begin traversing right on an easy ledge to several large trees. There is also a high version that allows a leader to protect the second: traverse right from the belay and step over to a sloping horn and good handholds. Finish the ledge traverse (75 ft.)
#3 Climb up and right to the north end of the ledge and climb the sloping flake/chimney (100 ft.).
#4 Walk right on the large summit ledge 100 ft to the final summit ridge. Many people simply scramble up the exposed 4th class section to the summit. If you are unsure of your ability, belay the final exposed section to the actual summit.
FA unknown
This is the easiest climb to the summit of the South Peak. On busy weekends this route is usually very crowded.

Routes #107-120 are located on the Cockscomb, the large pinnacle with the curved summit just north of Humphrey's Head. All Cockscomb routes end by climbing to the Windy Notch on the north side of the formation. From Windy Notch, climb the second pitch of WINDY CORNER (5.4) to the Summit Ledge.

107 FOGHORN LEGHORN 5.9 R
Start from OLD LADIES ROUTE, at the south edge of the Cockscomb.
#1   Staying directly on the arete, climb past a serious, runout section to a belay just below the level of PINE TREE TRAVERSE.
#2   Continue up the arete, past a spectacular finish, to the top.
FA Brian Rennex, Sandy Fleming 1986
Avoid the R protection rating by climbing only the second pitch.

108 COCKSCOMB OVERHANG DIRECT 5.9+
Start at the prominent block, at the top off the first pitch of OLD LADIES' ROUTE. The route ascends the narrow South Face of the Cockscomb.
#1   Climb the overhanging crack to the overhang above. Pull through the overhang and continue up easier rock to the summit of the Cockscomb. (100 ft.)
FA Mike Nicholson 1967
This route has been the scene of more than one major incident. Take big hexes and large friends.

109 COCKSCOMB OVERHANG DOUBLE DIR. 5.11d R
#1   Climb the face via thin, shallow cracks just left of C.O.D..
FA Greg Smith, Pete Absolon 1984

110 COCKSCOMB PINE TREE 5.3
Begin near the top of the first pitch of OLD LADIES' ROUTE, beneath the obvious chimney that splits the narrow south face of the Cockscomb.
#1   Climb through the chimney and out onto the West Face. Continue up a short crack to the north and belay at the ledge.(120 ft.)
#2   Climb to the summit, and then to the notch.
FA unknown

111 COCKSCOMB CHIMNEY 5.5
#1   Climb halfway into the chimney then head straight up past a left-facing flake to the top of the chimney.
#2   Move to the ledge with the dead pine.
FA unknown

112 HEARTBURN 5.6
The wide crack on the right margin of the west face of the Cockscomb can be used to make the start of COCKSCOMB PINE TREE a little more exciting.
FA Thais Weibel, George Livingstone 1967
Take at least one #4 Friend of other similar large gear.

113 COCKSCOMB PINE TREE TRAVERSE 5.3
From the ledge at the end of the first pitch of COCKSCOMB PINE TREE it is possible to make an easy but spectacular traverse straight across the top of the Cockscomb to the Windy Corner notch.
FA unknown

SOUTH PEAK-WEST FACE

114 COCKSCOMB OVERHANG 5.4

From the end of the chimney, move right until below the overhang. Climb the overhang to the top.

FA   Paul Bradt, Sam Moore, Don Hubbard 1939

FFA unknown

Routes 115-120 are on the west face of the Cockscomb

115 PARTIAL CANOPY 5.10d R

Start at the face just left and around the corner from the south-facing HEARTBURN flake.

#1 Climb the face tending slightly left to very thin cracks. Climb these to the top and move left to a ledge with a small tree and cold shuts. (85 ft.)

FA Greg Smith

Bring thin gear including plenty of micronuts.

116 HIT THE SILK 5.11a X

Begin 15 ft. to the right of BROKEN NECK.

#1   Climb the steep face, eventually treading slightly left to a thin crack. Climb the crack to a ledge and tree. (85 ft.)

FA Rob Robinson, Robyn Erbesfield 1984

Bring double ropes, a double set of RP's, tricams, and small TCU's.

117 BROKEN NECK 5.10b *

Begin below a vertical crack on the West Face of the Cockscomb, about 20 ft. to the right of the start of BREAKNECK. This direct start is hard to protect, and many climbers start farther left.

#1 Climb the crack nearly to its end. Move right a few feet and continue up the face to the ledge. Cold shuts. (80 ft.)

FA unknown

FFA Jeff Burns 1974

This is the old BREAKNECK DIRECT aid route.

118 BREAKNECK 5.6

Start at the center of the West Face of the Cockscomb, below a small birch tree.

#1   Climb the face to the tree. Traverse up and right until below a large left-facing flake. Climb up past the flake to a good ledge. (75 ft.)

#2   Climb up and right to a crack which is then followed left to the good ledge near the top. (50 ft.)

#3   Continue to the top or to the Windy Corner notch.

FA Ivan Jirak

To avoid heavy rope drag, do the small slab below the large flake as a short pitch or traverse in from the right (Luncheon Ledge).

119 JANKOWITZ-KAMM 5.5

(Var.) Just before the end of the first pitch a line of weakness can be followed up and left to Windy Corner notch.

FA   Jerry Jankowitz, George Kamm

Sandy Fleming on BROKEN NECK (5.10b). (Photo: Darell Hensley.)

120 TOTAL MALFUNCTION 5.11c **X**
Start just right of TRIPLE S.
#1   Climb the face to Windy Notch. (100 ft.)
FA   Greg Smith, Mike Cote 1985

121 TRIPLE S 5.8+ *
The left side of the West Face of the Cockscomb and the right side of the Face of a Thousand Pitons form a beautiful, steep corner. Start below the corner on a large ledge.
#1   Climb the corner to rappel hangers at a ledge below Windy Notch. (85 ft.)
#2   To finish, either climb the DIRECT FINISH or climb up to and do the last pitch of WINDY CORNER (5.4).
FA   Jim Shipley, Joe Faint 1960

Originally named Shipley's Shivering Shimmy, this route is now known to most climbers as TRIPLE S. This route is highly recommended.

122 TRIPLE S DIRECT FINISH 5.8
(Var.) This is the crack directly above the regular route. (50 ft.)
FA Chips Janger, Matt Hale 1968

The next 5 routes are located on The Face of a Thousand Pitons, the narrow south facing wall that merges with the left edge of the Cockscomb.

123 AGONY 5.10b *
About 15 ft. left of the TRIPLE S corner is an obvious crack/chimney system that splits the center of the wall. Begin on the large ledge just left of the start of TRIPLE S.
#1 Climb directly up to gain the main cracks. Climb the cracks to the overhang. Pull the overhang to a very uncomfortable belay in the narrow chimney. (90 ft.)
#2 Climb the narrow chimney to the top. (90 ft.)
FA George Livingstone, Tim Schenkle
FFA Matt Hale, Bob Lyon 1968
The short but difficult direct start was done by John Stannard in 1971. The original route traversed in from the right. The first pitch is nice, the second is a grunt.

124 MARSHALL'S MADNESS 5.9 *
Near the left side of the Face of a Thousand Pitons is another obvious crack/chimney system. Start on the large ledge beneath the face.
#1 Climb the steep cracks, past a small overhang, to a small blocky belay stance. Cold shuts. (40 ft.)
#2 Continue up steep cracks and chimneys until an easy traverse to the left is possible. Belay on the airy ledge on the outside corner of the face. Cold shuts. (75 ft.)
#3 Move back right and climb easy cracks and chimneys to the top. Cold shuts. (50 ft.)
FA Tom Marshall, John Christian, Andy Kauffman 1955

125 CRACK OF DAWN 5.10a *
#1 Climb the first pitch of MARSHALL'S MADNESS.
#2 Climb the second pitch of MARSHALL'S until it is possible to move to the right to a small overhang. Climb the beautiful jam crack through the overhang and up the face. The crack splits the face that is located between AGONY and MARSHALL'S MADNESS. (120 ft.) Cold shuts at the top allow a 165' rappel back to the base.
FA Marty McLaughlin, Eric Janoscrat 1980
One of the best routes at Seneca.

126 MONGOOSE 5.10a
Start below and 6 feet left of the start of MARSHALL'S MADNESS.
#1 Climb the finger crack on the outside corner of the Face of a Thousand Pitons.
FA Eddie Begoon, Pete Absolon

127 HORRENDOUS TRAVERSE 5.7

#1 Starting from the top of TRIPLE S, drop down about 15 ft., then traverse left across the Face of A Thousand Pitons to the small COTTONMOUTH ledge on the west corner of the face. The traverse is about level with the chockstone on AGONY.

#2 Continue traversing north on a small ledge to the large ledges of OLD MAN'S ROUTE.

FA John Christian, Bob Hinshaw 1959

FFA unknown

Maura Kistler on TRIPLE S (5.8). (Photo: Tony Barnes.)

FACE OF A THOUSAND PITONS

125

124   123

Routes #128-132 are located on the Snake Face. This face lies between the Face of a Thousand Pitons and NECK PRESS.

128 COTTONMOUTH 5.10a *
A few feet to the left of the outside corner of the Face of a Thousand Pitons, and on the West Face proper, there is a narrow right-facing dihedral. Start at the bottom of the dihedral.
#1   Climb the short dihedral until it is possible to move left to steep corners. Climb up through the steep, orange colored rock to a flat ledge. Cold shuts. (90 ft.)
#2   Step out right onto the Face of a Thousand Pitons and climb up to the belay block on the outside corner. Cold shuts.
#3   Move right and climb up cracks on the left side of the Face of a Thousand Pitons.
FA unknown
FFA Matt Hale, Tom Evans 1969
This classic old school, hard free climb was rated 5.9 for many years. Most people wish for a little more protection that can be placed from less arm-blowing stances. Its easy to get snakebit on this route. If steep and strenuous climbing is your poison, you'll like this one.

129 VENOM 5.10b *
#1   From the belay at the top of the first pitch of COTTONMOUTH step left and climb the right-facing corner/flake to the belay of MARSHALL'S MADNESS. (65 ft.)
#2   Move out left onto the West Face to reach a thin crack which splits the smooth wall. Follow the crack through the lichen to the top. (65 ft.)
FA Hunt Prothro, Herb Laeger, Charlie Rollins 1975

130 SIDEWINDER 5.11a *
Begin ten feet left of the start of COTTONMOUTH at a small right-facing corner capped by a roof.
#1   Climb the corner to the roof. Pull through the roof and move up the face until it's possible to make a scary traverse left to cold shuts (these are shared by NECK PRESS and a rappel route). (65 ft.)
#2   From the right edge of the belay ledge, climb straight up to a small roof. Surmount the roof and follow a small diagonal crack to a left-facing corner. Climb the corner and belay at the tree. (65 ft.)
FA Howard Doyle, Eric Janoscrat

131 BLACK MAMBA 5.12a
Start at the top of the first pitch of SIDEWINDER.
#1   Climb through the first bulge on the second pitch of SIDEWINDER and move up and right towards a face with three bolts. Make a short traverse right at the second bolt and climb up past another bolt and right-tending seams to the anchors on VENOM (70 ft.)
Note: Bring small TCU's and micronuts
FA: Tom Cecil, Ed Begoon 1992

132 THE VIPER 5.12b

Climb the second pitch of SIDEWINDER through the bulge. Diagonal up and right past a flake and thin crack, left of the bolts of BLACK MAMBA. Climb past a fixed pin to the top.

FA   Pete Absolon, Topper Wilson 1986

133 NECK PRESS 5.7

Begin about halfway between the outside corner of the Face of a Thousand Pitons and the large south-facing wall of LE GOURMET DIRECT START.

#1   Climb the curving, right-facing dihedral a few feet left of SIDEWINDER. At the top steep, awkward moves lead to a sloping ledge with a small tree and cold shuts (65 ft.)

#2   Step left and climb the back of the corner, encountering a strange off-width section and hand cracks near the top. Belay on the ledge at the south end of the Old Man's Traverse Ledge (65 ft.)

#3   The last pitch follows clean cracks in a corner to the right of the last pitch of OLD MAN'S ROUTE. (60 ft.)

FA   unknown

134 LE GOURMET DIRECT START 5.6 *

This popular pitch climbs the south-facing wall of the huge corner north of the Face of a Thousand Pitons

#1   Climb the left side of the south-facing wall. Move up to the right of one small tree and left of the second. Belay on the Old Man's Traverse Ledge. Beware rope drag and loose rocks at the top. (100 ft.)

#2-3   Finish on LE GOURMET.

FA   unknown

This route is somewhat awkward and is harder than it first appears.

135 THE BITE 5.9 **R/X**

Begin left of and just around the corner from LE GOURMET DIRECT START, beneath an inside corner.

#1   Climb the corner to a ledge with a small pine tree. (75 ft.)

#2   Continue straight up the face to the large ledge. (30 ft.)

FA   Chris Rowins, Chris Kulczcke 1979

136 LE GOURMET 5.4 *

On the west-facing wall around the corner from LE GOURMET DIRECT find a smooth, easy right-facing corner.

#1   Climb the corner 15 ft. until it ends. Follow the ledge to the left for 20 ft. to another, larger right-facing corner. Climb this to the tree on the LE GOURMET TRAVERSE ledge. Beware rope drag. (70 ft.)

#2   Traverse right from the tree and climb diagonally to the outside corner of the south-facing LE GOURMET DIRECT START wall. Climb the left edge of the wall and the arete to the vegetated platform. (100 ft.)

#3   Scramble up and left behind a large 4th class flake to the base of the prominent south-facing chimneys at the left side of the clean, 50 ft. Critter Wall.

#4   Climb the rightmost chimney and corner cracks to the top. (75 ft.)
FA Larry Griffin 1965

137 EASY OVER 5.5
(Var.) From the middle of the traverse on the second pitch, it is possible to climb straight up through an "S" shaped crack to the vegetated platform. (100 ft.)
FA Chris Schenk, Mark Reid 1975

138 LE GOURMET TRAVERSE (4th class)
This is a prominent ledge that splits the face from the vicinity of OLD MANS ROUTE to LE GOURMET. It affords an easy escape from several routes. There is one slightly tricky area near the north (left) end of the ledge.

The next three climbs start on the ledge at the top of the first pitch of LE GOURMET (FRONT C Face).

139 PROJECTED FUTURES 5.12b
Start 50 ft. right of the FRONT C corner, 30 ft. right of the bolt and pin of RONIN.
#1   Climb clean rock to the crack that starts about halfway up the face.
FA Pete Absolon
Bring many small brass or steel nuts. Double ropes are helpful.

140 RONIN 5.12d *
Begin near the right end of the LE GOURMET ledge, just left of PROJECTED FUTURES
#1   Climb the face to a bolt and piton. Move right into a finger crack. Climb the crack to intersect with OLD MAN'S ROUTE.
FA Mike Artz
FFAJohn Bercaw, Bill Dimsdale
Bring along micronuts for this one as well.

141 HISHIRYO 5.12C
Start just left of RONIN on the same ledge.
#1   Climb the face to the left of the bolt. Make a dynamic move to the bottom of the crack. Climb the thin crack for a couple of moves then reach left to a finger crack. Climb the crack to a ledge.
FA John Bercaw, Rod Hansen
Requires micronuts.

142 FRONT C 5.6 *
Directly behind the pine tree on LE GOURMET TRAVERSE ledge there is a prominent curving left-facing corner.
#1   Follow the corner up to the large ledge of OLD MAN'S ROUTE. (45 ft.)
FA Sayre Rodman

143 THE PLUM 5.9 X

Start on the LE GOURMET TRAVERSE ledge, about 10 ft. left of FRONT C.

#1   Climb the short wall to the right-facing corner. Climb past the corner to a short left-facing corner. Climb the corner and the wall above to a tree. (75 ft.)

FA Eric Janoscrat, Howard Doyle, Paul Anikis 1982

Eric Janoscrat: "A toss of the dice."

144 THE PEACH 5.8+ R

Begin on the LE GOURMET TRAVERSE ledge, 20 ft. left of THE PLUM and 5 ft. right of a thin flake system.

#1   Climb up a short wall to a small roof. Climb the roof then continue up the wall eventually heading slightly right. Follow good holds straight up the wall to the left-facing corner. Continue to a ledge.

FA Howard Doyle, Eric Janoscrat, Paul Anikis 1982

The protection is poor at the crux but improves higher up.

145 CAST OF THOUSANDS 5.9 R

Begin approximately 35 ft. left of the start of LE GOURMET, almost directly beneath the prominent rappel tree on LE GOURMET TRAVERSE ledge.

#1   Scramble up easy ledges to a short fingery wall leading to a small roof. Climb the wall straight up to the right side of the roof. Traverse left about 8 ft. until it is possible to pull up onto the steep white face. Climb the face to the LE GOURMET TRAVERSE ledge. (70 ft.)

#2   Climb FRONT C to the vegetated platform of OLD MAN'S ROUTE. (40 ft.)

#3   Scramble up and left to the leftmost of 3 large pine trees on OLD MAN'S ROUTE. Climb straight up a thin crack 8 ft. right of the tree to a left-facing corner. At the top of the corner move right then up to a belay at the base of the chimneys on the last pitch of LE GOURMET. (35 ft.)

#4   From the tree, step out left onto the lichen covered face. Follow the thin crack up and left to the base of a right-facing flake. Climb the flake and the face to the top. (50 ft.)

FA Bill Webster, Jay Hutchinson 1979

This is a combination of four separate one pitch routes. Other people involved were Bill Lepro, Sayre Rodman, Mark Thorne, Chris Lea, etc, etc.

146 CAST OF THOUSANDS DIRECT 5.9 R

(Var.) Climb straight up to the small overhang on the first pitch. (65 ft.)

FA probably John Stannard

147 PRUNE 5.7 *

Start: About 25 yards to the left of LE GOURMET, find a left-facing flake at about head level.

#1   Climb the flake and face to a low angle section that soon steepens. Climb the clean face past small ledges to the LE GOURMET TRAVERSE ledge. (100 ft.)

#2   In a direct line with the first pitch, climb cracks and blocks on the steep wall to a narrow ledge. Follow a left leaning finger crack through a clean wall to a good tree on the belay ledge on the traverse of OLD MAN'S ROUTE. (100 ft.)

#3   Climb the right-facing flake until it is necessary to step left. Continue up and right past finger cracks to a good belay. (60 ft.)
#4   Climb the left-facing corner to a flake. Follow the flake to the top. (50 ft.)
FA   John Christian, Arnold Wexler 1971
The inobvious and somewhat run-out first pitch (5.5) has caused route-finding problems. Locate a clean streak above a small curved birch tree and roots, midway between LE GOURMET and OLD MAN'S.

148 OLD MAN'S ROUTE 5.2
Start at several easy ledges leading up and right which lie on the far left side of the main West Face, before the cliff forms the huge Thais Corner.
#1   Scramble up easy ledges aiming for a large left-facing inside corner with a large black crack. Climb the crack and continue scrambling along an obvious path to the base of another chimney. (150 ft.)
#2   Climb the chimney. (20 ft.)
#3   Traverse out right on a long easy ledge (Old Man's Traverse Ledge) to the large vegetated platform. (100 ft.)
#4   Scramble up and right to the base of a steep corner. Climb the corner and pull over the chockstone to the top. (40 ft.)
#5   Walk through the obvious horizontal chimney to the Summit Ledge. Follow the ledge north to the final summit scramble. Rope up if necessary.
FA   Pim Karcher, Ken Karcher, Dick Gaylord, Bob Tieman 1949
At times this popular route is the scene of traffic jams. The upper part of the climb is also one of the standard rappel routes for the South Peak. At the start of the route remember to climb straight up at the initial easy ledges. The tendency to move right will place the climber off route on LE GOURMET TRAVERSE.

149 TRAFFIC JAM 5.7 *
Begin inside the chimney at the top of the last pitch of OLD MAN'S ROUTE.
#1   Climb the clean crack that splits the white, south-facing wall of the chimney. (40 ft.)
FA   unknown
Though short, a classic pitch.

150 LOW RISE 5.7
#1   Climb the wall directly opposite TRAFFIC JAM. The edge is off limits (15 ft.)
FA   unknown

151 ROAD KILL 5.7
#1   Climb the short face and crack 10 ft. right of the TRAFFIC JAM belay tree.
FA   Ron Dawson, Les Newman, Rick Scott

Routes #152-158 are located on (or just below) the Critter Wall.

152 CRITTER CRACK 5.6 *
Start 2 ft. right of the base of the LE GOURMET chimney (4th Pitch).
#1   Climb the hand crack close to a block at the left side of the wall. (Last pitch of LE GOURMET will be to your left). Continue up the hand and finger crack to the top. (45 ft.)
FA   Dave Garman, Mike Murphy, John Markwell 1972

153 CRISPY CRITTER 5.7 *
Begin 15 ft. right of CRITTER CRACK.
#1   Climb the thin crack. (50 ft.)
FA   Gary Aiken, Charlie Fowler

154 POOR MAN'S CRITTER 5.7
(Var.) Climb CRISPY CRITTER until it is possible to step left to another crack. Follow the crack to its end. (50 ft.)
FA   Gary Aiken, Steve Piccolo

155 CURLY CRITTER 5.9
Begin just right of the other Critter Cracks at an old pin about 4 ft. off the small ledge.
#1   Follow a hairline crack to the top.
FA   Cal Swoager, Bruce McClellan 1981

156 KOSHER KRITTER 5.10d
Start from a narrow ledge left of the Traffic Jam Chimney at the top of OLD MAN'S ROUTE.
#1   Climb the face past a bolt to a left leaning crack.
FA   Mike Perliss, Peter Absolon 1983
Micronuts protect the moves to the bolt.

157 KOSHER KRITTER DIRECT 5.9+
(Var.) Climb the face directly below KOSHER KRITTER, starting on the OLD MAN'S TRAVERSE LEDGE. 3 bolts protect the smooth face.
FA: Howard Clark, E. Begoon, Rick Fairtrace, Amy Clark, Tracy Ramm

158 CRUSHER CRITTER 5.9-
(Var.) Start below CRISPY CRITTER high on the OLD MAN'S Traverse Ledge.
#1   Climb the finger crack past a loose block. Finish at the start of CRISPY CRITTER. (40 ft.)
FA   Greg Collins, Hernado Vera

159 BACK TO THE FRONT 5.9 R
Start midway along the Old Man's Traverse Ledge, at a high point with small boulders.
#1   Climb a short right-facing corner. Traverse up and right to a bolt, and then continue past one more bolt and two fixed pitons. (100 ft.)
FA Dan Miller 1993
There is potential for a bad fall near the top of the route. A standard rack is necessary.

160 CONN'S WEST 5.3 *

The start is the same as OLD MAN'S ROUTE.

#1   Climb OLD MAN'S ROUTE until you are directly below an obvious left-facing corner/flake to the right of the offwidth corner crack of CLARKE'S CLIMB.

#2   Climb to the base of the corner by starting up the OLD MAN'S chimney for ten feet, then moving left. Or, climb the short, steep corner directly below the big flake (5.5). Continue up the corner crack to a loose ledge with a large tree. (60 ft.)

#3   Scramble up and right through the gully. Climb past several large chockstones to the top. (75 ft.)

FA   N.C. Hartz, Henry Schulter, Earl Richardson 1944

Use caution—there have been frightening instances of rockfall loosened by climbers on the ledge at the top of the second pitch.

161 CONN'S WEST DIRECT FINISH 5.4 *

(Var.) From the end of the middle corner/flake pitch, avoid the huge chimney by climbing the corner on the left. (50 ft.)

FA   Arnold Wexler

162 OUT OF THE COLD 5.10d

(Var.) Climb the crack and face just right of CONN'S WEST DIRECT FINISH.

FA   Pete Absolon, John Govi 1984

163 IRONY 5.4

(Var.) From the top of the first pitch of CONN'S WEST, climb the gully for 10 ft. then go straight up to the ledge. Follow the left-facing corner to the top.

FA   Pete Absolon, Linda Elleson

164 BY PASS 5.7

Start at the main corner/flake pitch of CONN'S WEST.

#1   Climb the main corner of CONN'S WEST for about 25 ft. until it is possible to angle up and left toward the roofs of WEST POLE. Continue to angle to the left and belay at the tree that marks the end of THAIS ESCAPE. (100 ft.)

#2   Climb a crack to the sloping ledge above, then move right and finish on WEST POLE DIRECT FINISH.

FA   John Markwell, John Christian, Arnold Wexler 1972

165 CLARKE'S CLIMB 5.9

Begin to the right of a small tree and large blocks that mark the start of WEST POLE.

#1   Climb the offwidth crack formed by the left-facing corner past several small trees and bushes to the right side of the WEST POLE roofs. (70 ft.)

#2   Move out right and up the wall to the West Face. Move up to the small tree above. (25 ft.)

#3   Diagonal up and left to the last pitch of WEST POLE. (25 ft.)

FA   A. Clarke, D. Kepler 1972

166 CLARKE'S CLIMB DIRECT FINISH 5.7

(Var.) Instead of moving back to the WEST POLE line, continue straight up the face to the tree.

Ron Walsh, Bruce Cox 1981

167 WEST POLE 5.7+ *

Climb the better part of the first pitch of OLD MAN'S ROUTE, then move left to a large ledge on the extreme left side of the main West Face. Belay at the tree which grows just to the left of the obvious double cracks.

#1   Follow the crack system up and then slightly right to small belay stance directly below the large double overhang. (70 ft.)

#2   Climb the crack directly through the double overhangs. At the top of the second roof, climb a left-facing corner to easier ground. Move up and right aiming for the obvious pine tree on a large ledge. (65 ft.)

FA George Bogel, Jim Payznski 1970

FFA Tim Beaman, Larry Myer 1971

An excellent route that sports an imposing roof of only moderate difficulty. The route is easier than it appears from the ground.

168 WEST POLE DIRECT FINISH 5.7

(Var.) To the left of the belay/rappel tree on the last pitch (also the top of CONN'S WEST DIRECT) is a steep corner/crack system. Climb this to the top. (50 ft.)

FA Joe Ebner, Dennis Grabnegger, John Markwell

169 SOLIDARITY 5.9

Use the same start as WEST POLE.

#1   Climb the first pitch of WEST POLE.

#2   Climb the second pitch of WEST POLE through the first roof. Traverse out left 20 ft. and then up 50 ft. to a belay.

FA unknown

170 GRANDIOSE 5.6

(Var.) This is a traversing line that connects WEST POLE with CONN'S WEST. Climb WEST POLE for about 50 ft. then start traversing right, past CLARKE'S CLIMB, across the face to the belay. (35 ft.)

FA Joe Faint, Jim Shipley

171 BRING ON THE NUBILES 5.9+ R *

This route starts 2 ft. left of the WEST POLE belay tree, near the arete formed by the intersection of the main West Face and Thais Face.

#1   Climb the short cracks up the face to an inverted V notch. Climb through the overhang then step left. Continue up to the THAIS ESCAPE ledge and belay.(130 ft.)

#2   Climb thin cracks in the West Face straight up to a small stance on a pedestal. Move up and right to very small horizontal cracks. Follow the cracks until situated on a blank face. Move left here at the crux, then climb up and slightly right to easier ground and the summit. (Do not move too far left around the corner except to escape the crux). Continue to the top. (110 ft.)

FA Hernando Vera, Kevin Stephens
The first pitch is run out. Many parties climb only the excellent second pitch, via
WEST POLE or CONN'S WEST DIRECT.

172 LOLITA 5.11a
Begin on the same face as BRING ON THE NUBILES, just right of that route.
#1   Using finger pockets climb the face.
FA Pete Absolon
Bring micronuts.

173 THAIS 5.5 *
The main West Face ends at the huge Thais Corner. THAIS climbs the right (north-
facing) wall of the corner. Start the climb near the right edge of the right wall.
#1   Climb the north-facing wall straight up to a belay at the base of a deep chimney.
(75 ft.)
#2   Climb the chimney and the crack above. Start angling slightly to the right and
belay at a ledge to the left of a crack. (110 ft.)
#3   Diagonal up and to the right in order to reach a sloping belay ledge on the out-
side corner of the face. (60 ft.)
#4   Move back left to the inside corner. Climb directly up to a rubble filled
gully/ledge below the South Peak summit. (60 ft.)
#5   Climb fourth class rock to the summit. (60 ft.)
FA John Christian, Bob Hinshaw 1954
A popular route despite its lack of exposure to sunlight. John Christian revealed the
origin of the name. The route is named after Thais, a prostitute in the opera of the
same name. After failing to seduce a monk she repented to a "straight and narrow"
path.

174 THAIS ESCAPE 5.2
(Var.) From the belay at the end of the 3rd pitch it is possible to escape off to the right
by heading for the belay tree shared by WEST POLE and CONN'S WEST DIRECT.
(40 ft.)
FA John Christian, Jim Shipley 1956

175 THAIS DIRECT 5.7
Begin directly below the huge Thais Corner.
#1   Climb the corner to a good ledge. (60 ft.)
#2   Continue up the corner to the blocky ledge at the right side of the PLEASANT
OVERHANGS roof.
#3   Continue climbing the corner, via an overhanging crack. After reaching a ledge,
move up and left for about 20 ft. to the rubble filled gully/ledge below the summit.
(110 ft.)
FA unknown

In 1972, a Fritz Wiessner route, THE BUTTRESS FINISH, was destroyed when the
entire upper section of the Thais Face fell to the ground.

176 DRESSING ROOM 5.11c
Begin just below the south summit left of the top of the Thais climbs.
#1 Pull the double tiered roof to the top. (25 ft.)
FA unknown
FFA Greg Smith 1987

177 PLEASANT OVERHANGS 5.7 *
Start directly below the huge slanting roof which starts at Thais Corner. Scramble up
easy ledges and establish a belay at a tree approximately 100 ft. to the left of the
Thais Corner.
#1 From the tree traverse out right to a corner squeeze chimney with a good sized
chockstone. After climbing the chimney, proceed up several overhanging corners,
aiming for the small ledge at the intersection of the roof and the Thais Corner. (100
ft.)
#2 Step off the ledge and begin to traverse out and left under the huge roof. At the
end of the roof, move up past a small overhang to an exposed and rather minuscule
belay stance. (100 ft.)
#3 Follow the left-facing inside corner straight up to easier terrain and a belay. (60
ft.)
#4 Scramble up to the summit. (30 ft.)
FA Jim Shipley and party
The first pitch is greasy when wet, run out, and a tad loose into the bargain. THAIS
DIRECT may be used as an alternate first pitch.

178 THE SORCERER 5.11a
Start at the top of the first pitch of PLEASANT OVERHANGS, or use THAIS
DIRECT to reach the same spot.
#1 Near the right end of the P.O. roof, pull the lip and climb the face above past four
bolts and gear placements.
FA Tom Cecil, Chris Clark 1992
Bring a rack of small and medium sized gear for the top.

179 DIRECT-TOE 5.10b R
Start below the P.O. roof at an obvious overhanging flake.
#1. Climb the flake that leans right to left. Follow it to the roof about 1/3 of the way
from its right end. (60 ft.)
FA Tom Evans 1966
FFA Howard Doyle, Matt Hale
Protection is difficult to place on the steep sections.

180 A BETTER WAY 5.9
Begin about 40 ft. left of the Thais Corner near a large tree.
#1 Scramble up and left to a ledge. Continue up and left to the top of a ledge system
and set up a belay by a small pine.
#2 Climb the lichen covered face to a dished out area. Move up a crack system
through a bulge. After the bulge, climb the face to a belay near the start of the big
pitch of GREEN WALL.

#3-4   Finish on GREEN WALL.
FA   Howard Doyle, Mike Whitman 1980

181 P.O. DIRECT FINISH 5.12b
#1   Climb the PO roof at its midpoint. From the pocket on the face, climb the face
above to a bolt. Climb the face to the right of the bolt then regain the crack. Follow
the crack to the top.
FA   Eric Janoscrat, Jim Lucas 1977
FFA Alex Karr

182 ALEX IN WONDERLAND 5.12a
#1   Climb the first pitch of P.O..
#2   Traverse out under the huge roof until 15 feet left of the aid route that surmounts
the roof.
#3   Pull the huge 15 ft. roof. Traverse right 25 ft. to good pins. Climb the crack to the
top.
FA   Alex Karr, John McKigney 1982

183 ARRESTED MENTAL DEVELOPMENT 5.9+
Start at the belay at the end of the second pitch of P.O.
 #1   Traverse the right wall of the corner, past a piton and onto the West Face, above
the roof. Move up the face past a bolt to thin cracks. Climb the crack to the top.
FA   Tom Cecil, Tony Barnes 1988

184 GREEN WALL 5.7 *
A beautiful white and green wall lies to the left of the PLEASANT OVERHANGS
roof. To the left of and below this wall, directly beneath the right edge of the
Gunsight Notch are two left-facing inside corners.
#1   Climb the innermost of the two corners to a spacious ledge. (25 ft.)
#2   Walk right for about 40 ft. to the base of a steep left-facing corner. Note: The first
two pitches are easily combined if the rope is directionalized against rope drag.
#3   Climb straight up the corner past several bulges and small overhangs to a good
sized belay ledge with some loose blocks. (100 ft.)
#4   Scramble up and right to the summit. (30 ft.)
FA   John Christian, Jim Shipley, Alan Talbert 1956
An excellent route on a beautiful face.

185 GUNS DO KILL 5.11a
#1   Climb the main pitch of the GREENWALL corner to a left-diagonalling crack.
Traverse left past one bolt to a left-facing corner. Climb the corner to a small roof.
Pull the roof to easy climbing above. Bolt anchor.
FA   Graham Dower, Rod Hansen 1993

186 GREEN DRAGON 5.10a **R**
#1   Climb the first pitch of GREEN WALL.
#2   From the small tree, climb the black, left-facing corner for about 30 ft. to the
roof. Traverse left to a crack. Move up the crack to its end, then climb the face on

small holds to the intersection with GUNSIGHT TO SOUTH PEAK. (85 ft.)
FA   Kris Kline, Eddie Begoon 1983

187 JADE 5.10a R
Use the same start as GREEN WALL.
#1   Climb the first pitch of GREEN WALL.
#2   Drop down slightly and traverse right 15 ft. past the GREEN WALL corner. Move out onto the face to an obvious vertical crack system. Climb the crack past a bulge and up through 2 scooped out areas to a second bulge below a left-facing corner. Climb the corner and continue through a small roof at the top of the corner. Wander up the face to the belay at the end of GREEN WALL. (100 ft.)
FA   Howard Doyle, Paul Anikis
The protection is difficult at the crux.

188 TOMATO 5.8 *
A few feet to the left of the two inside corners that start GREEN WALL there is an obvious flake leading to a ledge with trees.
#1   Climb the left edge of the flake to the ledge. (35 ft.)
#2   Step right and ascend the large left-facing corner. Climb straight up the dihedral to an intersection with GUNSIGHT TO SOUTH PEAK. Finish on that route. (120 ft.)
FA   Tom Evans, Matt Hale 1969

189 GUNSIGHT TO SOUTH PEAK 5.3 *
Start up in the Gunsight Notch, at its right (south) edge.
#1   Climb the arete towards the South Peak until it is possible to climb easy holds out onto the West Face. Diagonal up and right following cracks to a short chimney. Climb the chimney to a ledge that overlooks the East Face.(100 ft.)
#2   Move back right a few feet and climb up to the summit ridge. Walk, crawl, or slither your way across the narrow summit ridge to the register.
FA   Paul Bradt, Don Hubbard, Sam Moore 1939
Descent is usually made by downclimbing the short low angled slab on the southwest corner of the summit. This places the climber on the large Summit Ledge.

190 GUNSIGHT TO SOUTH PEAK DIRECT 5.4 *
Use the same start as GUNSIGHT TO SOUTH PEAK.
#1   Climb the arete on its East Face by using cracks and flakes to bypass the overhanging Gryphon's Beak.(100 ft.)
#2   Finish on GUNSIGHT TO SOUTH PEAK.
FA   Chris Scordoes and party

Routes #191-199 are located on the first short wall that is located below the Gunsight. Approach via the West Face trail.

191 BANANA PEELS 5.12b R

Begin just right of BANANA, at the rightmost of 2 birch tree, below a series of three horizontal cracks.

#1 Begin beneath a piton. Traverse left and then up and left 20 ft. to a flake and crack system. Then up to the top. The route finishes about 20 ft. left of the start.

FA Peter Absolon, Greg Smith

Finished with siege tactics. Bring friends, sliders, RP's, small tricams, and double 9 mm ropes.

192 FAT COUNTRY GIRLS 5.12c R

(Var.) Climb BANANA PEELS for 15 ft. then head straight up and out right on the wall past 3 bolts. Ends on the MANUAL DEXTERITY ledge. This is a more direct finish to BANANA PEELS.

FA John Bercaw, Rod Hansen

193 BANANA 5.6 *

Access to the Gunsight Notch is blocked on the West Face by a long low wall directly below the Notch. In the center of this wall is a distinct flake system.

#1 Climb the flake to the top. (25 ft.)

FA unknown

This route has some loose chunks.

194 BANANA DOWN UNDER 5.6

#1 Climb the first few feet of BANANA until it is possible to traverse left on a ledge. Climb the left-facing corner to the top.

FA Rick Fairtrace, Kathy Nardini 1983

195 LOX 5.8

Start directly below the rappel tree to the left of BANANA.

#1 Climb the roof and face directly to the rappel tree. At the top of the pitch angle slightly left of the rappel tree. (50 ft.)

FA Howard Doyle, Lori Larson

196 NOVA 5.8

To the left of and below the center of the Gunsight Notch is the short wall mentioned in the description of BANANA. Start below the crooked pine tree (used by many parties to rappel from the Notch).

#1 Climb the narrow left-facing corner straight up to the pine tree. (35 ft.)

FA Chris Kulczycki

197 BODYWEIGHT 5.9 R

Begin 15 ft. left of NOVA.

#1 Climb the face beneath the horizontal crack. Move through a broken section, aiming for the small tree. Pass the tree on its right side then continue straight up. (35 ft.)

FA Pete Timoch, Bernie Nypaver, Greg Edmonds 1983

Take a complete set of RP's.

198 SCRAMBLED LEGGS 5.8
Start to the left of NOVA at a large pine.
#1 Climb the wall to a series of right-facing flakes which start about 25 ft. up the wall. (40 ft.)
FA Eric Janoscrat, Jim LaRue, Susan Sands 1979

199 SHORT STUFF 5.8
Begin at the same large pine as SCRAMBLED LEGGS.
#1 Climb the face behind the tree.
FA Hunt Prothro, Howard Doyle

Routes #200-206 are located on the long ledge that lies below the Gunsight, and above the 9 previously listed climbs.

200 BURNING TENDONS 5.12a *
#1 Start 10 ft. left of the second pitch of TOMATO.
Climb the steep face past 3 bolts. (80 ft.)
FA Mike Cote, Mike Artz 1986

201 MANUAL DEXTERITY 5.10d *
From the end of the first pitch of TOMATO move left on the ledge until beneath a thin finger crack 10 ft. left of the leftmost pine tree.
#1 Climb the face and crack. (35 ft.)
FA John Bercaw, Greg Hand

202 DEBBIE 5.6
Begin 20 ft. left of MANUAL DEXTERITY.
#1 Climb cracks and flakes to a mantel move and sloping tree ledge below the Gunsight. (30 ft.)
FA unknown
A little done but enjoyable pitch.

203 SO WHAT 5.7
Start directly behind the small pine tree at the top of BANANA, at a flake with a piton at eye level, about 15 ft. left of DEBBIE
#1 Climb the flake and move right for about 20 ft.. Move back left and then up a ramp. Follow the ramp to a tree about 25 ft. below the Gunsight.(35 ft.)
FA Michael Ashe, Jeffrey Hallock 1982

204 BY THE WAY 5.9
Begin about 6 ft. right of PEDRO'S PROBLEM.
#1 Climb the flake system past an obvious horn to the top. (25 ft.)
FA Kris Kline

205 PEDRO'S PROBLEM 5.10c
Begin 50 ft. left of the start of MANUAL DEXTERITY, 15 ft. right of the rappel tree.
#1   Climb the crack. (20 ft.)
FA   Howard Doyle, Lori Larson

206 SLAMLINE 5.10d
Start just left of PEDRO'S PROBLEM.
#1   Climb the face just left of PEDRO'S PROBLEM. (20 ft.)
FA   Cal Swoager, Drew Bedford 1982

North Peak - West Face

As seen from the town of Seneca Rocks, this face is the expanse of rock that lies to the left of the Gunsight Notch.

Immediately left of the Gunsight is the Bell Wall, a steep orange expanse with both classic difficult cracks and quality bolted routes. This wall was also once known as the Movie Screen, though this name seems to have fallen out of use. All its one-pitch climbs are slightly overhanging and very sustained.

The left edge of the face merges into the hillside, allowing a Forest Service tourist trail to reach the summit of the North Peak. One striking feature cannot be seen until the climber actually stands at the base of the crag: the large smooth wall on the far left (known as the Euro Wall) is actually detached from the main crag, forming a huge fissure called No Dally Alley. The Euro Wall, identified by the huge inverted "V" roof, has some serious gear lines as well as a selection of good bolted climbs. The scramble to the base is steep and exposed.

BELL WALL AREA

Approach
The easiest way to reach the Bell Wall is from the blue-blazed West Face Trail. Follow the trail to its high point at the base of the short cliffband directly below the Gunsight Notch (you should have hiked past Thais Corner and the start to PLEAS-ANT OVERHANGS). Climb the ledgy and vegetated WEST FACE TO GUN-SIGHT NOTCH (5.0), which starts well left of BANANA where the wall is only about ten feet high. Or, do BANANA or another of the short climbs on the initial wall below the Gunsight (see South Peak - West Face).

The Bell Wall can also be reached from the South Peak-East Face, by climbing into and over the Gunsight Notch from the north end of Broadway Ledge (5.0).

Descent
The difficulty (and danger) of descent from the top of the Bell Wall has been eased by the placement of cold shuts or similar anchors at the top of many routes. SEE INDI-VIDUAL ROUTE DESCRIPTIONS FOR DISTANCES TO THE BASE. A single 185-200 ft. rope or two shorter ropes are necessary for a safe descent.

EURO WALL AREA

Approach
Follow the West Face trail to the area at the base of WEST FACE TO GUNSIGHT NOTCH. Continue walking north (left) until it's possible to scramble steep, exposed terrain up to the base of the middle of the Euro Wall. Most routes have anchors about eighty feet up and no second pitch, since the upper half of the wall (above the level of the distinctive CIRCUMFLEX roof) tends to be very loose.

Descent
Most recent Euro Wall routes are one-pitch climbs with fixed anchors. Always check pitch length in individual route descriptions if you intend to lower off. From the area above No Dally Alley it is possible to rappel from trees back to the West Face area near the south entrance of the Alley.

No Dally Alley routes are gained via the first pitch of WEST FACE TO GUNSIGHT NOTCH.

The following routes are on the Bell Wall.

207 PSYCHO FAGGOTS 5.11d R/X
Begin 15 ft. right of the prominent corner crack of MADMEN ONLY. This is the first route left of the Gunsight Notch
#1   Climb the crack and face. Take the upper crack at the split. Cold shuts (shared by MADMEN).
FA   Greg Smith, Mike Cote 1985
VAR.   A variation takes the lower crack (FA Cal Swoager 1985)

208 MADMEN ONLY 5.10a *
Start just to the left of PSYCHO FAGGOTS beneath an obvious right-facing corner crack.
#1   Climb up to a small stance at the base of the corner. Climb the crack for 60 ft. until it's possible to make moves into the wide crack on the right. Move up and find cold shuts on the right wall outside the crack. (80 ft.)
FA   Jim Shipley, Joe Faint
FFA George Livingstone, Roger Craig 1966
This was Seneca's first 5.10. Madwomen should also enjoy this excellent route.

209 PSYCHO KILLER 5.11b *
#1   Climb MADMEN ONLY to the point where the normal route traverses right. Continue climbing up and left eventually gaining a shallow right-facing corner. Climb past a bulge, then move up and left to the top. (95 ft.)
FA   Jack Beatty, Alex Karr 1981

210 PSYCHO DRILLER 5.12c *
Begin 30 ft. left of MADMEN ONLY.
#1   From the top of a big block follow the line of 6 bolts that lead up and left of PSYCHO KILLER. Cold shuts (85 ft.)
FA   Tom Cecil 1989
FFA Jim Woodruff

211 THE BELL 5.12a R *
Begin below the bell shaped arch located high on the wall midway between MAD-MEN ONLY and MALEVOLENCE.
#1   Climb the cracks to the base of THE BELL. Continue through the apex of the arch past a corner to a steep face. Ascend the face past a bolt to the top. (90 ft.)

The North Peak-West Face. Climber is visible on PSYCHO DRILLER (5.12).
(Photo: Jeff Bibb)

FA Cal Swoager, Alex Karr, Hunt Prothro, Mel Banks 1983
Everyone on the first ascent was an old man over the age of 30, wearing old style EB
climbing shoes. Serious, scary, and poorly protected.

212 THE MA BELL CONNECTION 5.11d
(Var.) Start by climbing THE BELL. Move left before the obvious corner and join
with MALEVOLENCE. Finish on MALEVOLENCE.
FA Greg Smith, Andrew Barry 1985

213 TOON TOWN 5.12
This bolted route was unfinished at this writing. The line goes up left of THE BELL
and through MA BELL CONNECTION.

John Govi on BANSAI (5.12b). (Photo: Darell Hensley)

214 MALEVOLENCE 5.10c *

Start about 60 ft. left of MADMEN ONLY, just to the right of a large boulder.
#1 Climb the crack and face to a small stance at a right-facing inside corner. Move up the corner for about 40 ft. to the end of the crack. Traverse right to a second, left-facing corner and then climb straight to the top. (100 ft.)
FA Hunt Prothro, Charlie Rollins 1974

215 MALEVOLENCE DIRECT FINISH 5.12b

(Var.) Instead of traversing right at the top of the narrow right-facing corner most of the way up MALEVOLENCE, go straight up past 3 bolts.
FA: Darell Hensley, Brian McCray, Tom Cecil 1992

216 IRRELEVANCE 5.10d

#1 Climb the first 50 ft. of MALEVOLENCE until it is reasonable to move left to an obvious left-facing inside corner. Climb the corner and the face above to the top of the cliff.
FA Jack Beatty, Greg Collins

The No Dally Alley flake and chimney.

217 BANSAI 5.12b *
Start left of MALEVOLENCE, just below a picturesque stunted pine.
#1   Climb the face past eight bolts to a cold shut anchor.
FA Tom Cecil, Darell Hensley 1992

218 SUMMERS EVE 5.10d X
Begin 30 ft. right of NEGATIVE FEEDBACK.
#1   Climb the shallow left-facing corner up and right to the top.
FA Pete Absolon 1984

A hard line has been top-roped between SUMMERS EVE and NEGATIVE FEED-
BACK.
FA Russ Clune 1994

219 NEGATIVE FEEDBACK 5.11a *
This route follows the major right-slanting feature 75 ft. to the left of MALEVO-
LENCE, just before easy ramps. Belay beneath a right-facing corner.
#1   Climb the corner for about 25 ft. to a ledge with a block. Continue up via a right
slanting corner/flake to a notch. Move past the notch onto the face. Move up and
slightly right to the top. (120 ft.)
FA Jack Beatty, Lieth Wain
Hooks have been used as protection just beyond the last good placements in the cor-
ner/flake.

220 HOOKED ON A FEELING 5.11c *
Start at NEGATIVE FEEDBACK.
#1   Climb the NEGATIVE FEEDBACK corner for about 25 ft. until it is possible to
clip a bolt. Climb left onto the face and move up past 3 more bolts to the top.
FA Tom Cecil, Sue Hartley 1988
Bring small wired nuts for the top.

221 SILENT BUT DEADLY 5.10c *
Scramble up the chimney until atop a ledge below and 15 ft. to the left of an obvious
finger crack.
#1   Climb the crack to the overhang, traverse left and belay. (40 ft.)
FA Howard Doyle, Lotus Steele 1976

The following routes begin below the Bell Wall and right of the Euro Wall

222 WEST FACE TO GUNSIGHT NOTCH 5.0
To the left of SCRAMBLED LEGGS there is a short face leading to a vegetated
ramp.
#1   Climb the short wall and follow the ramp up and left to the south entrance of the
No Dally Alley chimney. (150 ft.)
#2   Scramble back right over ledges to the base of the Bell Wall, and from there to
the Gunsight Notch.
FA unknown

223 OPTIONAL ILLUSION 5.12b *
Above the initial ramp of W.F.T.G.N.'s first pitch is a short smooth wall with two bolted climbs. This is the right hand climb.
#1 Climb the small right-facing flake past a horizontal crack then up the face. 4 bolts.
FA Ed Begoon 1990

224 THE WHOLE NINE YARDS 5.12a
Start just left of OPTIONAL ILLUSION.
#1 Climb the devious, crimpy face past four bolts. Cold shuts.
FA Darell Hensley, Brian McCray

225 NORTHWAY 5.0
Use the same start as W.F.T.G.N..
#1 Climb W.F.T.G.N. to the point where that route moves right. (150 ft.)
#2 Continue through the chimney and then up to the summit.
FA unknown
Not recommended.

226 PINE TREE TRAVERSE 5.0
Begin on the large ledge beneath the Bell Wall.
#1 Climb the vegetated ramp up and left to the summit.
FA Sally Chamberlin, Eleanor Tatge 1946

227 MISTAKEN IDENTITY 5.4
Begin outside the south entrance of the No Dally Alley chimney.
#1 Move up and right to the base of the left-facing inside corner. Climb the corner until it is possible to move left to a large ledge complete with a pine tree.
FA unknown

228 AMBER 5.10b/c
Begin about 20 ft. inside the south entrance of the Alley, on the east (main crag) wall.
#1 Climb a narrow right-facing corner to a ledge ten feet off the ground. Move up and left to another narrow right-facing corner, and continue over a bulge to the top. Protection is adequate but hard to place at the crux. (75 ft).
FA Howard Doyle, Stan Switala 1993

229 KAUFFMAN'S RIB 5.4
Begin at the south entrance of the No Dally Alley chimney.
#1 Climb the sloping south rib of the No Dally Alley flake to its top. Jump across the gap to the main rock. Loose rock near the top of the route. (140 ft.)
FA Andy Kauffman and party 1955

230 ONE STOP ?
Begin about 60 ft. inside No Dally Alley.
#1 Stem the chimney for about 60 ft. until it is possible to move south about 15 ft. to a belay ledge on KAUFFMAN'S RIB.
#2 Traverse back into the chimney and head straight up to the top of the flake.

FA Ed Worrell, Bill Hemphill 1954
Old Seneca guides gave this climb a 5.3 rating, but the exact location and the rating could not be confirmed.

231 NO DALLY ALLEY ?
Start inside the No Dally Alley chimney near an area of breakdown at its north entrance.
#1 Climb the east wall of the chimney to a lichen covered wall. Scramble to good ledges. (65 ft.)
FA John Christian, Ed Worrell, Bill Hemphill 1954
Nothing resembling the 5.3 reported in some old Seneca guides could be located.

The following routes are on the Euro Wall (the west face of the gigantic No Dally Alley Flake).

232 2ND TIME 5.6
This route starts at a slightly overhanging crack halfway between WEST FACE TO GUNSIGHT NOTCH and a pinnacle that marks INHERENT CONTRADICTIONS.
#1 Climb the crack about 40 ft. to a good stance. Climb right, around the bulge, to easier rock below an overhanging right-facing corner. Move through the overhang to join with WEST FACE TO GUNSIGHT NOTCH. (70 ft.)
FA Bruce Cox, Bob Bock, Al Moore 1982

233 INHERENT CONTRADICTIONS 5.10a R
Begin near the right (south) edge of the wall, just left of 2ND TIME. Scramble up to a ledge atop a small pinnacle, about 30 ft. off of the ground.
#1 From the ledge, move over the bulge to an inside corner facing right. Climb the corner until you can traverse left toward a detached column. Climb the face to the right of the column.
FA Howard Doyle, Eric Janoscrat
The route is characterized by difficult protection and loose rock.

234 BRAY NO MORE 5.12c *
Start 40 feet left of INHERENT CONTRADICTIONS, after scrambling to a point just left of a short right-facing corner in clean rock.
#1 Traverse right into the short corner, then climb up and slightly left past 6 bolts to a fixed anchor.
FA: Eddie Begoon 1992

235 BRAY TO THE LORD 5.12a
#1 Start 20 left of BRAY NO MORE and climb the face past 6 bolts to an anchor shared by BRAY NO MORE.
FA: Begoon, Howard Clark 1992

236 PSYCHO WARFARE 5.10c X
Start at a right-facing corner, 25 ft. right of the large detached flake that marks the start of CIRCUMFLEX, just left of BRAY TO THE LORD.

#1   Climb the right-facing corner to its end. Climb straight up the face to an over-hang. Traverse left for 15 ft. and join with CIRCUMFLEX. (100 ft.)
FA Eric Janoscrat, Howard Doyle 1981
The runout to the roof is frightening.

237 PRINCESS SNOWBIRD 5.11b *
Begin 10 ft. left of PSYCHO WARFARE, just right of and below the pointed, detached flake at the base of CIRCUMFLEX.
#1 Climb the face past five bolts to an anchor. (85 ft.)
FA: Tom Cecil, Eric Anderson

238 CIRCUMFLEX 5.9 * R
Start near the center of the west face of the No Dally Alley flake. Scramble to the top of the large pointed flake leaning into the wall.
#1   Climb a line of weakness that splits the face. Move up and right aiming for the large inverted "V" overhangs. Pull the roof just to the right of the apex of the inverted "V". Move up to a small belay at the base of a corner. (80 ft.)
#2   Climb the corner to the top of the flake. Loose. (35 ft.)
FA Dennis Grabnegger, Neil Arsensault 1974
There is a long runout on the wall below the overhang. Several good climbers logged considerable flight time after this one was put up.

239 THUNDERBOLTS 5.11d *
Start 25 ft. left of the start of CIRCUMFLEX.
#1   This route has 8 bolts. Climb the face past 4 hard-to-spot bolts. Pull the bulge moving right to gear placements. Continue up the face on the left past 4 more bolts to the belay.
FA Kenny Parker, Bill Moore, Kevin Parker 1987
The first bolt is up a bit, the next three hard to see. Take a 3.5 Friend and tricams.

240 THATS REALITY 5.12a X
Start 20 ft. left of THUNDERBOLTS.
#1   Climb a nondescript face (5.9 X) to a small right-facing corner about 15-20 ft. up. Clip a bolt then move out and right to another bolt. Continue up to a horizontal crack, then up past another bolt to a ledge. Continue left to a bolt belay.
FA Ed Begoon, Mike Artz, Kenny Parker 1988
The bolts are difficult to see.

241 SNICKERS 5.10d
Begin at a large tree about 60 ft. to the left of the start of CIRCUMFLEX.
#1   Climb right-facing corners and flakes for about 35 ft. Continue up a small right-facing corner which is somewhat broken. After passing several pins the corner ends. At this point traverse to the right about 6 ft. to a crack. Continue past several over-hangs to a "V" notch in the large roof. Pull the roof and move up to a ledge. (100 ft.)
FA Jim Marshall, Pete Moore
FFA Howard Doyle, Eric Janoscrat 1978
This route requires a large rack. The first ascent party had to climb in unison due to

the length of the route and the absence of ledges. Double 165 ft. ropes are recommended. Expect some bad rock and difficult route finding.

242 Name Unknown ?
A route up a right-facing corner and the face to the left of SNICKERS has been done by Greg Smith and partner. Details have been lost to the passage of time and other adventures.

243 UP FRONT 5.3
Start about 50 ft. to the right of the north entrance of the No Dally Alley chimney.
#1 Climb a diagonal line left to right following a broken, lichen covered face. Traverse right about 5 ft. on a vegetated ledge, then climb a 10 ft. crack on the West Face. (This crack is 5 ft. left of the inside corner facing left.) Scramble up to the north end of the No Dally Alley flake. (70 ft.)
#2 Climb the ridge on the flake to the chockstone that forms a bridge to the North Peak.
FA June Lehman, Linda Harris 1971

The next three routes are located on the short wall that lies above the No Dally Alley flake and directly below the North Peak summit.

244 PLANET GONG 5.6
Begin at the obvious left-facing inside corner directly below the North Peak summit.
#1 Climb the corner to the ledge. (30 ft.)
FA Johnny Robinson, Sandy Fleming, Barbara Fox 1982

245 FLYING TEAPOT 5.7
Start 20 ft. left of PLANET GONG.
#1 Climb the flakes to the ledge. (30 ft.)
FA Johnny Robinson, Sandy Fleming 1982

246 TALK DIRTY TO ME 5.8
Start 35 ft. left of PLANET GONG.
#1 Climb flakes to a ledge. (30 ft.)
FA Sandy Fleming, Johnny Robinson 1982

LOWER SLABS

From the town of Seneca Rocks the Lower Slabs are visible as the lowest cliffband below the North Peak. This area, though completely visible from the road, escaped exploration and development until well after the rest of Seneca experienced intensive new route activity. The prevailing rumor for many years was that the rock was low angled and loose. Some Lower Slabs faces do have extensive vegetation and loose flakes, and others are somewhat slabby compared with the rest of Seneca. But some great routes do exist. The less intimidating scale and less strenuous techniques required on the more kicked-back climbs offer a refreshing change. Trails are steep with little flat or solid terrain.

APPROACH
Approach the classic routes on the north end of the slabs by taking the 1.7 mile tourist trail that leads to the observation deck on the North Peak. Continue about 120 yards past the half-way marker which is on a signpost with an interpretive plaque about iron ore. Instead of following the next switchback left, follow the blue blazed trail south-southeast into the woods toward the North Peak.

If you are already on the upper Seneca crags, it is best to descend on the West Face Trail to the base of the steep rock steps at the top of the Hemlock Grove talus. Hike north, skirting the base of short walls which eventually become the Lower Slabs. You will cross the field of debris left by the Gendarme's collapse in 1987.

All Lower Slab routes are described north to south (left to right).

DESCENT
It is possible to walk or scramble back around to the base of the routes on the north end of the Slabs. Bushwhacking off from the top of Slab routes farther south is arduous. There are no permanent rappel anchors along the top of the Slabs. If you find it preferable to rappel from your chosen climb, make sure your ropes reach the ground!

Routes #247-249 are located on a detached band of short smooth walls that lie downhill and north of the prominent Lower Slab cliffband visible from the valley floor.

247 FIRE ON THE MOUNTAIN 5.9
Start about 150 ft. left of FOR SLAB RATS ONLY directly behind an oak tree and just right of a right-facing corner.
#1   Climb the hairline crack that splits the wall.
FA Ron Dawson 1984

248 FOR SLAB RATS ONLY 5.8
Walk to the right side of the west face of the detached cliff. About 20 ft. before the right edge of the cliff, is a clean right-facing corner on a ledge.
#1   Climb the hand to finger size crack up the corner. (40 ft.)
FA Mike Cote, Don Womack

249 ANGRY ANGLES 5.10d **R**
Locate the pin and bolt on the extreme right edge of the detached cliff.
#1   Climb the fine face and right edge to the top. (45 ft.)
FA   Greg Smith, Mike Cote
It is advisable to tie off the pin which sticks far out of the rock. There are only two fixed protection points but they are right where you need them. The bolt needed replacing as of this writing in 1994.

The remainder of the Lower Slabs routes are located on the main wall, and are described north to south (left to right). Routes #249-254 are located to the left of the obvious SCUTTLE crack and east of routes #246-248.

250 PENATOIDAL MEMBRANES 5.5
Begin at the left end of the wall.
#1   Climb the crack and left-facing corner to the top. (25 ft.)
FA   Eric Janoscrat, Paul Anikis 1982

The narrow right-facing corner has been toproped.

251 THE WARLOCK 5.9 *
Start at a small tree on a tiny ledge formed by the base of a right-facing flake. This climb is just left of the obvious finger crack of DISCREPANCY, and fifteen feet right of MEMBRANES.
#1   Climb the thin crack system, tending right at the top to merge with the more obvious DISCREPANCY. (50 ft.)
FA   Paul Anikis, Eric Janoscrat 1982

The face between WARLOCK and DISCREPANCY has been toproped.

252 DISCREPANCY 5.8- *
Begin at an obvious finger-sized crack that splits the face at its highest point.
#1   Climb the crack to the top. (55 ft.)
FA   Drew Bedford, Jim Howe 1981
A Lower Slabs classic.

253 AUTUMN FIRE 5.11c *
Start 15 ft. right of DISCREPANCY at a very thin crack that slants right to left.
#1   Climb the crack, angling up and left to a small ledge. Climb straight up the broken face and over a downward facing flake to the top. (60 ft.)
FA   Howard Doyle, Paul Anikis

254 DEATH BY ABUNGA 5.9 **R**
Begin 8 ft. left of the obvious SCUTTLE crack.
#1   Climb the face to the top. (30 ft.)
FA   Paul Gillispie, Chris Guenther, Topper Wilson 1983

Rick Templeton on DISCREPANCY (5.8). (Photo: Bill Webster)

255 SCUTTLE 5.5
Start at a prominent vertical crack with a short, wide section. A small tree grows about 10 ft. up the crack.
#1 Climb the crack to the large tree at the top. (50 ft.)
FA unknown

256 SELDOM SEEN 5.7
Begin 20 ft. right of the SCUTTLE crack.
#1 Climb the face to a very narrow, right-facing corner. Continue to a ledge then move right to the base of a narrow left-facing corner and flakes. Follow the system to the top.
FA Mark Thesing, Paul Anikis

257 R2D2 5.5
Start around the corner, 40 ft. right of SCUTTLE at two large right-facing corners and a large detached flake.
#1 Ascend the right side of the flake. (120 ft.)
FA Jim Lucas, Len Sistek

258 SUMMER BREEZE 5.10b
Begin 20 ft. left of the TIPS flake (a detached blade of rock protruding from the ground inches from the wall) at a right- facing corner formed by two overhangs.
#1 Climb below the small overhang until it is possible to traverse left to the corner. Undercling 20 ft., across the smooth wall, up and right to a small tree on a ledge. Continue up the corner until it is possible to move right to a large ledge with trees. (75 ft.)
FA Chris Guenther, Topper Wilson 1983
Steep, strenuous, continuous, and a little loose at the top.

259 TIPS 5.10a R
Start at the second wall to the left of the large right-facing corner. Begin at a large, loose, pointed detached flake which lies only inches from the main wall.
#1 From the top of the pointed flake, move up the face for about 8 ft. to an undercling. Move left and up to a small flakey crack. Continue up the crack to a small overhang. Move right and up a small right-facing corner to the top.
FA Howard Doyle, Paul Anikis 1982
Protection is somewhat poor and difficult to place. Take plenty of small wired nuts.

260 IT AIN'T THE MEAT, ITS THE MOTION 5.4
Begin around the corner from TIPS at a right-facing corner.
#1 Climb the left side of the corner using cracks and the narrow chimney with chockstones. (40 ft.)
FA Rick Fairtrace, Barbara Bates, Cathy Nardini

261 ADRENALINE 5.10a **R**

Use the same start as SNAKEBITE.

#1   Climb the shallow right-facing corner to an undercling. Climb left and up a short left-facing corner. From the top of the corner, move up and right toward a pine tree and the belay. (85 ft.)

FA Paul Anikis, Mike Artz 1983

Take a skyhook.

262 SNAKEBITE 5.7

Start to the left of GOOD MORNING at a gully angling up and left. Scramble up to the second tree.

#1   Climb the flake to the right of the tree until it ends. Move left and climb the wall straight through the small overhangs and up to the pine tree on top. (75 ft.)

FA Rick Fairtrace, Glenn Thomas, Barbara Bates

263 4 ME 5.4

Use the same start as GOOD MORNING.

#1   Climb the grungy chimney in the right-facing corner. Step out right and pull the small overhang. Continue up the face to the top. (80 ft.)

FA Jim Lucas, Len Sistek

264 GOOD MORNING 5.7

Begin at the huge, obvious right-facing corner in the middle of the cliff. This corner can be seen from the road.

#1   Move up the corner, past overhanging flakes. Pull the overhang, then continue past a short chimney to a large tree at the top. (140 ft.)

FA Eric Janoscrat, Denny McDonough 1977

265 WITCH WAY 5.10c

Use the same start as GOOD MORNING.

#1   Climb a large pedestal up the light colored face. Follow the overhanging crack to the roof. Pull the roof on its right side. (50 ft.)

FA Paul Anikis, Eric Janoscrat, Howard Doyle 1982

The protection is good, though difficult to place.

266 AND GOD CREATED ALL MEN EQUAL 5.10c

Start underneath the largest roof, just right of GOOD MORNING.

#1   Climb the large, inside right-facing corner to the large overhang. Using horizontal cracks, pull the center of the roof. Continue up a loose, easy, unprotected face to the top. (90 ft.)

FA Greg Collins, George Flam 1981

The roof is a small body length.

267 SUNNY DOWN BULOW 5.9

Traverse right to left under the slabs until past DARK STAR and almost to GOOD MORNING. Cut back south across a ledge to a ramp. Climb the ramp to a spacious ledge. At the left side of the ledge is a right-facing corner with a tree about 25 ft. up.

#1 Climb the face just right of the corner. Move past a bush then traverse right to another right-facing corner. Move up this corner and around to the right of a thin right-facing flake. Move straight up, passing the finish of PRAYING MANTLE. (90 ft.)
FA Eric Janoscrat, Howard Doyle, Pannil Jones 1983

268 PRAYING MANTLE 5.9
Start just right of SUNNY DOWN BULOW.
#1 Climb up and slightly right on loose flakes to a short right-facing corner. Move up and over the large flake, past a bush, and into right-facing corners. When the corners end, go up and left to the large pine tree.
FA Eric Janoscrat, Howard Doyle, Mark Thesing 1983

269 GUILLOTINE 5.9
Start right of PRAYING MANTLE on the same ledge at a pine tree.
#1 Climb the flake and the short corner. At the end of the corner move left to right-facing corners. Climb up to the gaping guillotine shaped rock in the overlap. Climb the left side of the rock and then up right on flakes. Traverse right to a small pine. (90 ft.)
FA Howard Doyle, Eric Janoscrat, Lori Larsen, Mark Thesing 1983

270 DARK STAR 5.11c R
Begin about 80 ft. right of the huge right-facing corner, at the small alcove which becomes a right-facing corner.
#1 Climb the right-facing corner to a larger right-facing corner. From the top of the second corner traverse up and right under roofs to a pine tree at the top. (75 ft.)
FA Paul Anikis, Howard Doyle
The protection is difficult. This condition is compounded by some bad rock.

271 CAPTAIN HOOK 5.9+ R
Start from a ledge 20 ft. left of SENECA SAMURAI.
#1 Move up the face to a right-facing corner and flake system. Pull over the small overhang and then up to the top. (100 ft.)
FA Paul Anikis, Cal Swoager, Eric Thesing, Mark Thesing
This is a good route, though the flake is hollow. Take a skyhook.

272 SENECA SAMURAI 5.9
Start from a ledge about 15 ft. off of the ground and left of a large vegetated left-facing corner.
#1 Climb left to the pine tree. Climb straight up a very shallow corner to the roof. Move right at the roof, then up the corner to the top. (80 ft.)
FA Cal Swoager, Eric Janoscrat 1980

273 KNOW FEAR 5.10c R
There is a bolt to the right of SENECA SAMURAI, a short distance above the ledge.
#1 Climb to the bolt and up to a short right-facing corner. There is a poor TCU placement in the corner and another bolt near its top. (70 ft.)
FA Ed Begoon, Mike Artz, Howard Clark and David Clark 1991

274 GRASS SNAKE 5.11a
Fifteen feet right of KNOWN FEAR and twenty feet left of the vegetated corner, find three bolts on the face to the right of a left-arching seam.
#1 Climb on thin edges past the three bolts and up to placements for small to medium camming gear. Pull the bulge and continue up easier ground to a tree. (50 ft.)
FA Ed Begoon, Tony Barnes 1991

275 FINGER LICHEN GOOD 5.6
Start about 15 ft. left of WAP SUCK at the obvious layback flake.
#1 Climb the flake. Move up about 40 ft. to the end of the crack. Continue up a blocky, lichen-covered face. Turn the corner and finish by mantling a vegetated ledge. (45 ft.)
FA Josh Stark, Phil Wilt 1983

276 WAP SUCK #4 5.5
At the far right side of the Lower Slabs there is a right- leaning, vegetated corner with a dead tree.
#1 Ascend the right-leaning corner to the top. (45 ft.)
FA Eric Janoscrat, Jim McAtee, Bill Lepro 1978

277 WAP SUCK DIRECT 5.5
#1 Climb the face to the right of the corner, intersecting the route at its midpoint.
FA Eric Janoscrat, Jim McAtee, Bill Lepro 1978

Adam Erlich on POLLUX (5.10a). (Photo: Darell Hensley)

SOUTH PEAK - EAST FACE

In general, the East Face of the South Peak of Seneca is smoother and more expansive than the West Face, with continuous moderate routes and excellent hard face and thin crack climbs. The face is especially attractive during the cooler months when the east-facing rock bakes in the morning and early afternoon sun.

The South Peak-East Face can be separated into three distinct areas. The Southeast Corner rises in a gigantic triangle from the south edge of the East Face. All the routes on the Southeast Corner end on Lower Broadway Ledge or on the top of the South End. Another area of rock extends from the east side of the Humphrey's Head area, above Lower Broadway, north to Windy Notch and Upper Broadway Chimney. The third and largest portion of the South Peak-East Face is the main east face which rises from Upper Broadway Ledge.

APPROACH

Southeast Corner— Walk east 50 ft. past the culvert carrying Roy Gap Run under the road and find a blue blazed trail on the left. (Please do not hike up the eroded scree slope above the culvert pipe.) This trail forks almost immediately, with the right branch leading up to the area at the base of SKYLINE TRAVERSE (Lower East Face Trail) and the other left under the toe of the Skyline Buttress and up to the TOTEM-CANDY CORNER area.

Broadway Ledge— Except for Southeast Corner routes and several short climbs that start from the OLD LADIES' traverse, almost every other South Peak East Face route originates from the Broadway Ledge. The complete Broadway Ledge extends from the top of the South End to a point just short of the Gunsight Notch.

Access to Lower Broadway Ledge is obtained in one of the following ways:

Do a climb on the Southeast Corner or South End.

Or, skirt the end of the crag above the South End: Hike up the West Face Trail to Luncheon Ledge, at the base of Humphrey's Head. Walk south from Luncheon Ledge past a short downclimb to a large east-facing tree ledge atop the South End. This is the south end of Lower Broadway.

Upper Broadway can be reached from here by walking north to a short chimney with a large chockstone (Lower Broadway Chimney). Continue along the easy ledge to another steep section. (Upper Broadway Chimney, 5.2). At this point it is also possible to step right and climb fourth class rock to narrow tree ledges. Some parties rope up for this section since a slip would likely result in the climber's death. Continue scrambling until it is necessary to head up through the trees to reach the base of the main East Face (you will be below DIRTY OLD MAN and just right of the bottom of the OLD LADIES rappel route).

From Roy Gap Road it is possible to hike and scramble to Upper Broadway (and the East Face of the North Peak). The trail to Upper Broadway follows a small ridge parallel to and about 80 yds. east of the East Face (this is the old Scramble Trail to the North Peak). The trail follows small fin-like outcroppings of sandstone, is more resistant to erosion, and out of rockfall range. Take Roy Gap Road 80 yds. past the culvert pipe in the Gap and find blue blazes at a steep cut in the road bank on the left. Climb up and right and follow the trail to a point a little over halfway to the top and just about even with the Gunsight Notch. Take a feeder trail (blue arrow and blazes) heading left (west) to 3rd and 4th class ledges. After an initial 10 ft. rock step, hike directly up to head for LICHEN OR LEAVE IT, etc., or left and up about sixty vertical feet to Upper Broadway. The path from the end of the feeder to Broadway is unmarked and follows ledges and exposed terrain.

DESCENT

There are three main rappel routes from the Summit Ledge of the South Peak back down to Broadway, where any of the described approaches can be reversed.

1) In order to reach the south end of Upper Broadway, start at the large pine located at the far southeast corner of the Summit Ledge. This pine tree is located almost directly over Windy Notch. Rappel down the East Face to the pine tree located at the end of the second pitch of OLD LADIES' ROUTE (70 ft.) Rappel from this tree to reach Broadway (60 ft.). Two ropes will place you directly on Broadway Ledge in one rappel.

2) Fifty feet north of the OLD LADIES' rappel just described it is possible to use a large tree to descend to fixed anchors at the top of the first pitch of Frosted Flake (75 ft.). From here it is 50 ft. to the ground. Two ropes will place you directly on Broadway Ledge in one rappel.

3) To rappel from the South Summit proper to Upper Broadway, locate a small keyhole notch about midway along the summit ridge. It lies roughly above GREEN WALL as seen from the west and above ALCOA PRESENTS on the east face. In the keyhole notch is a rock horn with slings. It is 165 ft. to Broadway from the notch. Sixty feet directly below the rock horn there are fixed rappel anchors on the ALCOA-CONN'S EAST ledge; 65 ft. lower is another pair halfway up the first pitch of CONN'S EAST DIRECT. If you only have one 150 ft. rope it is necessary to make three rappels.

There are cold shuts above HIGH TEST and NIP AND TUCK, just below the north end of the South Summit ridge. These are 105 ft. above Upper Broadway.

To reach the East Face Trail from Upper Broadway, locate the initial downclimb near the base of CASTOR and POLLUX. Follow narrow ledges to the north and down, until you reach the trail.

Rappelling down from the central part of Broadway Ledge to the very base of the East Face using trees is possible but you will not find maintained fixed anchors. Rappelling down to the base of the WORRELL'S THICKET area from Lower Broadway is also possible (165-185 ft.), although you must set your own anchors or set ropes directly around trees.

It is possible to rappel down the West Face after doing South Peak-East Face climbs. See the DESCENT information for the South Peak-West Face.

Some experienced climbers downclimb OLD LADIES' ROUTE from the Summit Ledge. However, a slip from most positions on this route would most likely result in the death of the climber. In addition, on crowded weekends the route is used continuously.

Check individual route descriptions for the presence or proximity of fixed anchors.

Descents from several areas on the South Peak deserve special mention. Humphrey's Head is generally descended by scrambling down via the north ridge (5.0) or rappelling its west face from fixed slings around a block. The best descent for the Cockscomb is to climb the last pitch of WINDY CORNER, then use either the East Face or West Face rappel routes, to reach the ground.

Routes #278-289 are located on the Southeast Corner. Approach these routes by using the trail along the base of the East Face.

278 SKYLINE TRAVERSE 5.3 *
The climb begins at a chimney, in a right-facing corner, about 25 ft. to the right of the outside (south) edge of the Southeast Corner. First climb a short wall (5.3) to a wide ledge with trees.
#1   Climb up the chimney and corner to a good ledge. Climb the left-facing corner to a horizontal crack. Move left a few feet to an airy ledge at the intersection of the South End and the East Face. A very old pair of eye bolts mark this belay. (100 ft.)
#2   Step off of the belay ledge and make very exposed moves to the left in order to reach a wide chimney. Climb the chimney then angle up and left to a good tree growing from a slab. (70 ft.)
#3   Continue up the chimney and crack to its end at the south end of Broadway Ledge. AVOID THE LOOSE GULLY at the top of the pitch by stepping right early to solid rock and a trail. (50 ft.)
FA   Paul Bradt, Don Hubbard, Sam Moore 1939
This is one of the finest routes of its grade. The start of the second pitch has filled the hearts of many beginning climbers with fear. The position is airy but the protection is excellent. USE CAUTION: there is a large amount of loose rock at the top of the climb—and some of Seneca's most popular routes are directly below you. In fact it is unwise to be at the base of YE GODS, DROP ZONE, and CANDY CORNER without a helmet.

279 OLD TIMER'S LUCK 5.8
Start at the beginning of the second pitch of SKYLINE TRAVERSE.
#1   Continue up the corner crack on the right side of the chimney where SKYLINE moves left and up the ramp. Climb the steeping crack to the top of the South End.
FA   Don McIntyre, Dan Kearney 1993

280 HERO PENDULUM 5.5 R
Start at the end of the first pitch of SKYLINE TRAVERSE.
#1 From the belay ledge, move right around the large block to a horizontal line of weakness. Follow this to WORRELL'S THICKET. (110 ft.)
FA David Kepler, George Pinkham

281 CAPTAIN TRIVIA 5.8 R
Begin 15 ft. to the left of the DUFTY'S POPOFF corner, beneath a broken overhang.
#1 Leave the SKYLINE TRAVERSE belay ledge and move right until below the overhang. Climb the face, passing through the overhang on its left side. Continue up the face and merge with DUFTY'S at the roof. Finish on the normal route. (130 ft.)
FA Leith Wain, Matt Lavender 1978
The protection is poor at the crux.

282 DUFTY'S POPOFF 5.7 R *
Start a few feet to the right of the end of the first pitch of SKYLINE TRAVERSE, at a large block.
#1 Move right to the base of the prominent left-facing inside corner. Climb the corner past orange colored rock to an overhang. Step right over the roof and climb the face above to the top. (130 ft.)
FA Art Gran, Bob Dufty 1959
A nice climb with an exciting crux. The easy face above the roof has sparse protection.

283 DUFTY'S POPOFF DIRECT 5.9 R
(Var.) Beginning below and right of the normal start, climb a crack to a tree. Move left to join with DUFTY'S POPOFF.
FA Cal Swoager, Greg Phillips 1980
This line is rarely done and may be sparsely protected.

284 KAUFFMAN-CARDON 5.4
Use the same start as DUFTY'S POPOFF.
#1 Move right from the belay until at the DUFTY'S POPOFF corner. Climb the right wall of the corner then traverse right across the buttress to easier climbing. Continue to a tree. (100 ft.)
#2 Traverse right on ledges until it is possible to move up to Broadway Ledge. (75 ft.)
FA Andy Kauffman, Betty Kauffman, Joan Ascher, Phil Cardon 1954

285 BEE STING CORNER 5.7 *
(Var.) At the end of the first pitch of KAUFFMAN-CARDON it is possible to climb a large left-facing corner. (75 ft.)
FA George Livingstone, Arnold Wexler, Andy Kauffman

286 CARDON'S RIB 5.4 R
(Var.) From the end of the second pitch of KAUFFMAN-CARDON, step right and then climb straight up the arete and east face of the BEE STING CORNER (50 ft.)
FA Phil Cardon, John Christian 1970

287 THE TOMATO THAT ATE CLEVELAND 5.9

Begin on the same ledge as the start to SKYLINE TRAVERSE, a few feet to the right of the chimney.

#1   Climb the thin right-tending cracks to a larger crack and a tree. Move past this to the start of the DUFTY'S POPOFF corner. (45 ft.)

#2   Climb DUFTY'S POPOFF.

#3   Walk left to the steep arete overhanging the ledge. Climb the arete. (40 ft.)

FA   A. Clarke, D. Kepler, D. Mong 1973

288 H&H 5.7 R

Begin directly between SKYLINE TRAVERSE and WORRELL'S THICKET.

#1   Climb the broken face aiming for the prominent corner of BEE STING. About midheight on the first pitch climb just to the right of a prominent roof. Belay at the base of BEE STING CORNER. (100 ft.)

#2   Move left on the ledge until it is possible to climb the face above. Move through a small overhang, step left and climb the face above. (60 ft.)

FA   Herb Laeger, Howard Doyle

The route is poorly protected. A better protected variation of the first pitch goes through the overhang.

289 WORRELL'S THICKET 5.0

About 150 ft. uphill (north) of the southeast corner is a long, vegetated, low angled ramp.

#1-#2   Climb the right-leaning ramp in two easy pitches, until Lower Broadway Ledge is reached. (160 ft.)

FA   Ed Worrell, Blondie Worrell

Routes #290-296 are located on the East Face of the Cockscomb and all start on the easy traverse ledge on the second pitch of OLD LADIES'. See the description of OLD LADIES' in the South Peak-West Face section of this guide. OLD LADIES' starts on the West Face, but soon passes through a notch at the intersection of Humphrey's Head and the Cockscomb, onto the East Face. All variations are on the East Face.

290 DIANE 5.8 R

Begin approximately 10 ft. to the left of I.O.W. below a small overhang.

#1   Climb through the overhang to a flaky, brown face. Step left to a narrow, severely overhanging arete. Continue up the arete to a shallow chimney. Follow the crack to the top. (90 ft.)

FA   Chris Kulczycki, Steve Schneider, Chris Rowins 1979

291 INCREDIBLE OVERHANGING WALL 5.11a R *

Begin about 20 ft. to the right of the start of the second pitch of OLD LADIES' below an arching crack.

#1   Climb the face and arching crack up the overhanging wall to a no-hands rest. From there move right 10 ft., then up the lichen covered wall to the top. (90 ft.)

FA   Greg Hand, Mel Banks 1976

292 GIBBS EXCELLENT ??
Begin about 3 ft. to the left of the pine tree which grows in the center of the second pitch of OLD LADIES' ROUTE.
#1   Climb the face over the bulge to a fixed pin. Continue up the face. (90 ft.)
FA   Chris Rowins, Steve Schneider 1979

293 COCKJOB 5.7
Begin just to the right of GIBBS EXCELLENT and almost directly behind the small tree that grows only inches from the rock.
#1   Climb the face and thin crack up and right until it merges with DISCONTENT. Finish on DISCONTENT. (80 ft.)
FA   Chris Rowins, Chris Kulczycki, Steve Schneider 1979

294 WINDY CORNER 5.4
Begin from the large pine at the end of the second pitch of OLD LADIES' ROUTE.
#1   Climb the cracks that lead up to the Windy Corner notch that separates the Cockscomb from the main South Peak. From the ledge climb cracks through an over-hang to the Summit Ledge. (45 ft.)
FA   unknown

295 JANE'S ROUTE 5.2
Use the same start as WINDY CORNER.
#1   Climb the large left-facing corner/flake that lies just to the right of WINDY CORNER and just left of the OLD LADIES' ROUTE chimney. (40 ft.)
FA   Jane Showacre

296 AMAZING GRACE 5.7 **R**
Start at the end of the second pitch of OLD LADIES.
#1   Traverse straight out right from the belay on easy ledges to a tree. (35 ft.)
#2   Climb to about 15 ft. from the top of the second pitch of DIRTY OLD MAN. (60 ft.)
#3   Traverse up and right across the East Face until it is possible to drop down on top of the Soler Flake. (120 ft.)
FA   Larry Conrad, Mike Schmitt 1974
This route has several long runouts.

The remainder of the South Peak-East Face routes begin from the Broadway Ledge. Routes #297-305 begin from the lower part of Broadway Ledge near Humphrey's Head or below Old Ladies Traverse Ledge.

297 WIND UP 5.5
Start at the first significant outcrop at the south end of the Broadway Ledge.
#1   Climb the right-facing corner/flake up and right to a ledge. Follow the left crack to the top. (70 ft.)
FA   Jessie Guthrie, Tom Whitesol 1974

298 REVERSE C 5.1

From the south end of Broadway Ledge walk to a point about 20 ft. from the left side of the east face of Humphrey's Head, just right of the start of WIND UP. Begin below a shallow rotten flake.

#1   Climb the REVERSE C flake up to the top of the small formation below and left of Humphrey's Head.

#2 Continue up the south ridge of Humphrey's Head.

FA   Bob Gephardt, Cliff Alexander 1957

299 ABSOLUTELY WORTHLESS 5.8 **X**

(Var.) Climb REVERSE C up to the first traverse. Continue straight up loose blocks.

FA   Cal Swoager, Teri Porter 1980

300 HIGH TECH 5.9

Start beneath Humphrey's Head at an orange face.

#1   Climb the thin crack which angles left. (50 ft.)

FA   Parker Hill, Hernando Vera 1981

The protection is good, but difficult to place.

301 A CHRISTIAN DELIGHT 5.3 *

Begin directly below Humphrey's Head.

#1   Climb up a steep white wall to a good stance below another white wall. Move left around a bush then move up and to the right. Climb up to the notch between the Cockscomb and Humphrey's Head. (140 ft.)

FA   John Christian and party 1970

302 UP AND COMING 5.4

Begin near the right edge of Humphrey's Head.

#1   Climb the face and left-facing inside corner. Work up and right, aiming for the large ledge at the base of the south face of the Cockscomb. (130 ft.)

FA   June Lehman, John Christian, Sally Greenwood 1970

The route is easily broken into two pitches if desired.

303 LADY ELAINE 5.4

Begin from the Broadway Ledge, just above the short chimney that breaks the ledge (Lower Broadway Chimney).

#1   Climb the face up and right in order to reach a crack. Follow the crack for about 30 ft. until it is possible to traverse to the right across a lichen covered face. Aim for a ledge with a small pine tree. From the ledge move left on small ledges to easier ground. Continue to the Cockscomb Notch at the end of the Old Ladies Traverse and belay. (120 ft.)

FA   Mark Thorne, Ray Friend, Earl Devault

304 ANGEL'S WING 5.9- **X**

Begin 15 ft. left of HIGHWAY TO HELL.

#1   Climb straight up from the bottom to a stance 10 ft. left of the first bolt on HIGHWAY TO HELL. Trend up and left.

FA Cal Swoager, Eric Janoscrat, Terry Ivanhoe
No protection worth speaking of. Take hooks.

305 HIGHWAY TO HELL 5.10a **R** *
Start 15 ft. left of the steep step that interrupts the Broadway Ledge.
#1 Climb the face to a small overhang. Move past the overhang to a blank looking face. Ascend the face past two bolts to easier ground. (80 ft.)
FA Eric Janoscrat, Cal Swoager
The two bolts may be the only protection worth anything on this route. Serious.

306 EXPLETIVE DELETED 5.7
Start below the Upper Broadway Chimney. Begin from the top of a mound of debris.
#1 Climb the wide crack to a ledge. Move up and left to intersect with OLD LADIES' ROUTE near the left side of the Cockscomb. Traverse right and belay beneath the DISCONTENT crack. (85 ft.)
#2 Climb DISCONTENT for a few feet until it is possible to move right to a small orange crack. Follow this flake and crack up and right. Easier ground leads to the summit of the Cockscomb. (90 ft.)
FA Dan Taylor, Todd Eastman 1974

Routes #307-355 begin from the Upper Broadway Ledge or are alternate pitches that start high on the cliff.

307 DISCONTENT 5.4
Start from the top of the steep step that breaks the Broadway Ledge. Begin just left of an obvious curving flake.
#1 Climb the broken face and crack to the left of the flake. Belay on the ledge that runs beneath the Cockscomb. This ledge is also the second pitch of OLD LADIES' ROUTE. (35 ft.)
#2 Climb the face aiming for an obvious orange crack. Climb the crack and face to the top. (85 ft.)
FA Rich Pleiss, Bill Webster 1974

308 DINAH MOE HUM 5.9+ *
Start below a thin crack and short arete at the right edge of a smooth face. The route goes up just right of the obvious shallow corner.
#1 Climb the face and thin cracks on the outer edge. (45 ft.)
FA Jessie Guthrie 1975

309 RAPPEL DOWNS HORSERACE 5.7 **R**
This route starts at the base of the main rappel route that begins on the south end of the Summit Ledge.
#1 Climb the flakes that angle slightly left. Pull the small overhang and climb straight up to the rappel tree.
FA Eric Janoscrat, Cal Swoager, Howard Doyle 1981
Not recommended on weekends.

310 DEEP THROAT SUNDAY 5.9- R
Start between DINAH MOE HUM and DIRTY OLD MAN, just left of RASP.
#1   Climb right-facing flakes for 20 ft. then move right for about 7 ft. onto a lichen covered face. Climb straight up.
FA   Eric Janoscrat, Cal Swoager

311 RASP 5.8 R
Start about 10 ft. left of the DIRTY OLD MAN corner.
#1   Climb the face to the top.
FA   Howard Doyle, Paul Anikis, Eric Janoscrat

312 DIRTY OLD MAN 5.6 *
Begin beneath an obvious left-facing flake that lies approximately 6 ft. off of the ground and about 40 ft. to the right of Upper Broadway Chimney. This is the left side of the exfoliating plate that forms FROSTED FLAKE on the right.
#1   Climb the face to a small ledge beneath the flake. Climb the flake then move right to a good belay. (60 ft.)
#2   Climb up and left toward a steep left-facing corner. Climb the corner to the Summit Ledge. (75 ft.)
FA   Charlie Fowler, Jon Harris, Dave Bushman 1973

313 ICING ON THE CAKE 5.11d
Begin 40 ft. left of FROSTED FLAKE and a few feet right of DIRTY OLD MAN.
#1   Climb the wall past 2 bolts to a ledge (50 ft.)
FA   Pete Absolon 1988

314 PUT A WIGGLE IN YOUR STRIDE 5.11d
Start just left of FROSTED FLAKE.
#1   Climb the face past 4 bolts. (50 ft.)
FA   Eddie Begoon, Daniel Miller 1988

315 FROSTED FLAKE 5.9- *
Start to the right of DIRTY OLD MAN at a thin right-facing flake. The flake arches up and right and ends at a small overhang.
#1   Climb the crack to the overhang. Step right and move over the bulge, then back left to a small belay ledge. Cold shuts (45 ft.)
#2   Climb up and right to a corner. Climb the corner for about 10 ft. then move left onto the face. Climb over a series of bulges to the top. (75 ft.)
FA   Jim Callahan, Linda Connelly, Brock Baker 1974

316 KID GALAHAD 5.9
(Var.) Climb the first pitch of FROSTED FLAKE as normal. Climb straight up the orange face past a bolt to good holds.
FA   Gary Hahn, Chris Rice, Josh Rice
Protection is somewhat sparse.

317 T.R. RAP AND TAP 5.11d
Start about 20 ft. right of FROSTED FLAKE at a block leaning against the wall.
#1   Climb through an orange streak in the smooth wall and continue up past a small right-facing corner. Six bolts to cold shuts.
FA   Mike Perliss 1985
This old death-route was retro-bolted in 1994.

318 MISTER JONES 5.11b/c *
Start on the large sloping ledge about 30 ft. left of SOLER.
#1   Climb the face past 7 bolts to shuts. (80 ft.)
FA   Eddie Begoon, Mike Artz 1988
Very sustained.

319 BROTHERS IN ARMS 5.12b
Start 15 ft. left of SOLER.
#1   Climb the face past 7 bolts to a small roof. Climb the roof to a flake. Finish at a small pine.
FA   John Bercaw, John McGowan 1988
Stick clip the first bolt. Bring a #4 Friend.

320 SOLER 5.7 *
Begin at the obvious, quite large, left-facing flake that aims for the true summit of the South Peak.
#1   Climb the steep corner until it curves right and forms a ledge. Belay below an orange ramp, or move 15 ft. right to cold shuts. (135 ft.) There is a runout about 30 ft. up where the flake forms a wide crack, unless you bring a piece six inches or larger.
#2   Climb the ramp that leads to a small left-facing corner in the overhang above; if you belay from the shuts, scary 5.7+ face climbing leads up to the aforementioned corner. Climb through the notch then follow cracks up the face. At the point where the crack system suddenly ends, climb up and left on face holds to a good ledge which appears just when its needed. Follow the crack up and right to the very summit of the South Peak. (140 ft.)
FA   Tony Soler, Ray Moore 1951
The second pitch is spectacular, a great achievement for 1951.

321 SOLER ESCAPE 5.5
(Var.) At the top of the first pitch of SOLER, climb out and left to the base of a grungy looking orange crack. Climb the crack past the overhang to a tree. Climb past the tree to the Summit Ledge. (75 ft.)
FA   unknown

322 NATURAL MYSTIC 5.10d/11a
Start at the cold shuts located just right of the top of the first pitch of SOLER.
#1   Make bouldery moves to a bolt, then climb over a slight bulge past two more bolts and gear placements. Cold shuts.
FA   Tom Cecil, Tony Barnes
If you blow the first few moves you're likely to deck out on the ledge below.

323 TALBERT PICKLEFISH 5.9- R

Begin at the end of the first pitch of SOLER.

#1   Downclimb the flake until it is possible to traverse out left to the obvious crack. Move left about 8 ft. to reach the crack. Follow the crack straight up and finish between 2 trees. (90 ft.)

FA Dennis Grabnegger, Dick Miller 1973

324 PICKLERIGHT 5.9

(Var.) Climb the crack until it is possible to move to the right. Move up to the Summit Ledge. (120 ft.)

FA Jeff Burns, Randy Gainer 1973

325 TERMINAL VELOCITY 5.10b R

Start approximately 10 ft. right of the SOLER flake and about 6 ft. left of the CONN'S EAST corner beneath a small left-facing corner.

#1   Climb the face, past the left-facing corner, up incipient cracks for about 25 ft. to a horizontal crack. Move right and up, using a small flake, into small lichen-covered cracks. Follow the cracks up to and over a bulge. Continue up to a belay. (75 ft.)

#2   Finish on any other route.

FA Howard Doyle, Marty McLaughlin, Eric Janoscrat 1979

The route has one runout section.

326 TERMINAL ATROCITY 5.10c X

(Var.) A direct start to TERMINAL VELOCITY. Climb the face just right of TERMINAL VELOCITY. On the first ascent protection was placed from CONN'S EAST.

FA Pete Absolon, John Govi 1985

327 TIME FLIES 5.11a R

The start is the same as CONN'S EAST.

#1   Climb the first few feet of CONN'S EAST then move up and right over the moderate face to a bolt. Climb the face past 2 more bolts to the top of the SOLER flake.

FA Howard Clark, Mike Artz, Eddie Begoon

Take RPs or HBs and #0 TCUs.

328 CONN'S EAST 5.5 *

Start at a prominent left-facing corner system 20 ft. right of the SOLER flake.

#1   Climb the leftmost short corner up and right to a chockstone in the main flake. Pull over this and continue up the huge flake. It's possible to get off route on a steep 5.7 lieback variation. The regular route goes right past ledges and a small tree to the chimney behind the flake. Go up this, then traverse right along the top of the flake until easy progress is barred by a small corner and slightly overhanging wall. Cold shuts. (130 ft.) Some parties belay below the chimney to avoid rope drag.

#2   From the end of the ledge, move out right onto the steep, exposed face. Move up and right over a bulge to welcome buckets. Traverse right twenty feet to a bolt anchor below ORANGEAID and ALCOA. (50 ft.)

#3   Traverse easily to the right to an arching left-facing crack formed by a large flake. Climb the crack to the base of a chimney. Move past the large chockstone into an easy gully and up to a large ledge (80 ft.)

#4   Step right then up to the summit. Walk the ridge south to the summit blocks. (100 ft.)

FA   John Stearns, George Kolbucher, Bob Hecker, Jim Crooks 1944

329 HOPEFUL ILLUSIONS 5.10d

The start is the same as the CHANGELING.

#1   Climb the face to the left of the corner to a small right-facing corner. Above the corner, climb the face via shallow cracks. At this point the bolts on the CHANGELING are about 10-12 ft. to the right. From the end of the cracks move up and left to a small bush. Climb a left-facing corner then move up to CONN'S EAST. (90 ft.)

#2   Finish on CONN'S EAST.

FA   Howard Doyle, Eric Janoscrat 1979

330 HOPEFUL ILLUSIONS DIRECT FINISH 5.11d R

(Var.) When the cracks end, continue straight up to a flake at the extreme right hand side of the small overhang. Then continue straight up to the top of CONN'S EAST flake.

FA   Kris Kline 1983

331 THE CHANGELING 5.11c *

Start below a shallow right-facing, right-leaning flake, approximately 35 ft. to the right of CONN'S EAST.

#1   Climb the flake for about 40 ft. to its end. Move up past two bolts and a crack to the roof. Traverse left around the roof and up to a belay on CONN'S EAST. (90 ft.)

#2   Finish on CONN'S EAST.

FA   Jack Beatty, Jim Woodruff 1979

332 CHANGELING DIRECT FINISH 5.11b R

(Var.) Finish through the roof, using the shallow right-facing corner on the right.

FA   Greg Smith 1985

333 TERRA FIRMA HOMESICK BLUES 5.11c *

Begin just left of the twin cracks of CASTOR and POLLUX at a short but obvious right-facing corner.

#1   Climb the corner to its end then step left to a crack. Follow the crack until you are forced into thin face moves. Crank the crux and continue up to a horn. Continue up the crack to cold shuts. (120 ft.)

FA   Herb Laeger, Eve Uiga 1975

Small wired stoppers and TCUs protect this excellent route. There is a long runout above the crux.

334 CASTOR 5.10a *

Approximately 75 ft. north of the SOLER flake and just left of CONN'S EAST DIRECT START there are two cracks splitting the wall. CASTOR is the left crack.

#1   Climb the crack to the ramp. (45 ft.)

#2 Climb the ramp to its end, then continue up to cold shuts at the end of the first pitch of CONN'S EAST. (75 ft.)

#3 Climb straight up from the belay over moderate rock to the summit. The 5.9-crux is somewhat thinly protected. (90 ft.)

FA Pat Milligan, George Livingstone 1971

Most people climb only the first pitch, although the last pitch is good. The 5.10 climbing ends after 15 ft.

335 CASTOR TO TERROR 5.10b

(Var.) Climb CASTOR for 30 ft. until you can angle up and left toward the large crack at the top of TERRA FIRMA. Finish on TERRA FIRMA.

FA Kris Kline

Not much new rock, but still an interesting route.

336 POLLUX 5.10a *

Start at the right crack.

#1 Climb the crack to the ramp. (40 ft.)

#2 Rappel off or follow another route to the top.

FA Pat Milligan, George Livingstone 1971

There is a flexy flake at the crux.

337 CONN'S EAST DIRECT START 5.8 *

Begin near the north end of the Broadway Ledge, beneath a diamond shaped block 10-15 ft. above the ground. Directly above the block is an obvious shallow chimney.

#1 Climb the difficult face to the block. Above the block, climb the crack to a good ledge. Step right from the ledge and climb a short left-facing corner to a ramp. Ascend the ramp up and to the right to a good ledge. Walk back left on the ledge to a tree. (110 ft.)

#2 Finish on pitch #3 and #4 of CONN'S EAST.

FA Arnold Wexler 1954

The first few (crux) moves are quite committing.

338 Unnamed 5.11d/.12a

Start at the belay at the top of the first pitch of CASTOR and POLLUX.

#1 From the belay step right and climb a narrow left-facing corner, protecting as well as possible. Climb the sphincter-clenching face above past three bolts, moving up and right past a seam to the CONN'S EAST/ALCOA belay ledge.

FA Ed Begoon, Howard Clark 1990

339 TRIPE FACE BOOGIE 5.9+

(Var.) Climb CONN'S EAST DIRECT START for about 15 ft. until one can step left to a crack. Climb the crack to the first good ledge. Finish on the normal route.

FA Dieter Klose, Savvy Sanders 1977

340 BOGTROTTER 5.9 X

(Var.) From the first good ledge about 40 ft. up, step left and climb the face aiming for the ledge at the start of ORANGEAID. (50 ft.)

FA Marty McLaughlin, Mike Endicott 1977

341 GRAND FINALE 5.9+ *
Start from the good ledge at the end of the second pitch of CONN'S EAST.
#1 Traverse 15 ft. left of the prominent ORANGEAID finger crack along the easy ledge. Climb up through the shallow right-facing corner, then angle left to the summit. (90 ft.)
FA Eve Uiga, Herb Laeger
The route is somewhat committing at the bottom and a little run out at the top—a good route for those comfortable at the grade.

342 ORANGEAID 5.10b *
Start just left of the bolt anchor at the end of the second pitch of CONN'S EAST.
#1 Climb the orange cracks up to the roof. Surmount the roof then move up easier rock to the summit. (125 ft.)
FA Mark Carpenter, Barry Wallen 1966
FFA John Stannard 1971

343 GATORADE ??
A route up the very thin seams between ORANGEAID and ALCOA was led by Greg Smith, probably with at least a little aid.

344 ALCOA PRESENTS 5.8 *
Begin on the same ledge as ORANGEAID.
#1 Climb the cracks just right of the bolt anchor to a narrow overhang. Climb the shallow right-facing corner and face above to a notch in the summit ridge. (100 ft.)
FA Joe Faint, Mike Nicholson
FFA Tom Evans, Bob Lyon, Bob Williams 1968
An enjoyable route that tempts many into standing on a pin. As you pass, note the solid aluminum piton after which the route is named.

345 THE VISION 5.6
Begin on the same ledge as ORANGEAID.
#1 Climb the face about 10 ft. to the right of the tree, aiming for orange colored rock. Climb the orange rock up and to the left aiming for the summit. (95 ft.)
FA D. Klose, N. Maynard
Instead of moving left it is also possible to climb a 5.7 crack to the right.

346 VIETNAM VETERANS AGAINST THE WALL 5.11b
Begin from a small block located about 10 ft. right of CONN'S EAST DIRECT START.
#1 Climb the face up and right, aiming for a small yellow area of blocky rock. Continue up and left following shallow cracks until they end. When slightly above a bush on the left, traverse left to a crack system. Move up the crack and merge with CONN'S EAST. (65 ft.)
FA Marty McLaughlin, Cal Swoager 1981
This route probably deserves an "R" protection rating if you're not expert with micronuts.

347 SPOCK'S BRAIN 5.11a *
Start just to the right of V.V.A.W. at a right-facing corner.
#1 Climb the corner up to thin cracks. Follow the crack system up to a shallow, strenuous ramp. Follow the ramp up and left to cold shuts just below the CONN'S EAST DIRECT flake. (100 ft.)
FA Leith Wain, Jack Beatty 1979
Take small wired nuts and TCUs.

348 HIGH TEST 5.9+ *
Begin about 35 ft. to the right of CONN'S EAST DIRECT START below a sickle shaped ledge.
#1 Climb shallow cracks and knobs to the sickle shaped ledge. (25 ft.)
#2 Move right on the ledge to the left-facing corner. Climb the corner until it is possible to move right to shallow cracks. Climb the cracks to face moves below an overhang. Protect this area well. Climb the steep right-facing corner to a good stance. Follow cracks and flakes to the top. (120 ft.)
FA Herb Laeger, Eve Uiga 1974
An excellent route that offers much variety. Double ropes are useful if you want to make it in one pitch.

349 HEAVY FUEL 5.12c
Use the same start as HIGH TEST.
#1 Climb the first 20 ft. of HIGH TEST and step left onto a narrow ledge. Climb up past four bolts to the ledge.
FA Ed Begoon, Darell Hensley, Tom Cecil

350 UNLEADED 5.9+
Use the same start as HIGH TEST.
#1 Climb the first 80 ft. of HIGH TEST to the right-facing corner. Traverse left 15 ft. to a ledge.
#2 Step back onto the face and climb straight up, then slightly right to a left-facing flake. Climb slightly left via a thin crack.
FA Hunt Prothro, Howard Doyle
This route can be done as a single pitch.

351 NITRO 5.10d
(Var.) Begin 10 ft. left of LOW OCTANE and about 7 ft. right of HIGH TEST. Climb the thin seam, that is not quite a crack, to the sickle shaped ledge.
FA Cal Swoager, Mike Artz 1983
The protection is thin.

352 LOW OCTANE 5.11b *
(Var.) Climb a shallow crack system just to the left of NIP AND TUCK. This merges with HIGH TEST at the traverse past the sickle shaped ledge.
FA John Bercaw, Jim Nigro

353 TICKET TO RIDE 5.10c
Use the same start as LOW OCTANE.
#1 Climb flakes just right of LOW OCTANE. Move right to gain a crack. Follow the crack through an 8 inch overhang and climb up to intersect with NIP AND TUCK. At the crux of NIP AND TUCK step left to an undercling at a roof. Pull through the roof into a lichen covered crack. Climb cracks to the bolt at the summit. (135 ft.)
FA Mike Artz, Eddie Begoon 1983
Try to protect the first 30 ft. as well as possible.

354 NIP AND TUCK 5.10c *
Begin atop the large block at the extreme north end of the Broadway Ledge.
#1 Start from the right end of the block and climb very thin cracks up and left. Follow the crack system through the overhang and on up to the top. (140 ft.)
FA Herb Laeger, Eve Uiga 1974
FFA Bob Richardson, Rich Perch, Herb Laeger 1974

355 EAST FACE TO GUNSIGHT NOTCH 5.0
Begin at the extreme north end of the Broadway Ledge.
#1 Climb up and right over easy rock to the Gunsight Notch. (30 ft.)
FA unknown

356 GUNSIGHT NOTCH EAST 5.5
This route does not start from the Broadway Ledge. Begin from ledges directly below the Gunsight Notch attained by scrambling from ground level.
#1 Climb directly to the notch passing a few very old pitons. (60 ft.)
FA Paul Bradt, Sam Moore, Don Hubbard

The next 3 routes climb a wall below Upper Broadway Ledge, directly below the start to SOLER.

357 PRAYING TO THE ALIENS 5.8 **R**
Begin 75 ft. left of LUNGE OR PLUNGE, just 5 ft. right of an easy scramble.
#1 Climb a shallow left-facing corner/flake to the ledge.
FA Mark Thesing, Ed McCarthy 1983

358 LUNGE OR PLUNGE 5.11d
Locate an orange and white wall directly below the start of SOLER.
#1 Climb the left-facing corner and the face above. Move past a bolt to the Broadway Ledge.(60 ft.)
FA Howard Doyle, Eric Janoscrat
Cal Swoager was the lunger and plunger.

359 DC 5.9 **X**
This route also starts below the Broadway Ledge, just right of LUNGE OR PLUNGE.

#1 Climb a nice 5.8 crack studded with old army pins to a ledge.
#2 Move up and right past horizontals. Run it out to the Broadway Ledge.
FA Pete Absolon, M. Armbrecht 1988

Eddie Begoon on HEAVY FUEL (5.12c). *(Photo: Tony Barnes)*

NORTH PEAK - EAST FACE

The North Peak - East Face is a low, broken face that lies high on the hill. The face possesses little visual appeal, but contains many excellent routes. On crowded days this is the best area to visit if you wish to escape the throngs draped over the South Peak routes.

APPROACH

There are two hiking approaches to the face. Many parties walk up the North Peak tourist trail to the top, at the north end of the rocks. From here locate the base of the East Face trail and follow it down.

Another good approach is to hike up the Scramble Trail, which climbs the slope east of the rocks. Hike through Roy Gap and continue up the road about 80 yds. Locate a blue blazed trail on the left which follows a small rocky ridge parallel to the East Face. At a point about even with the Gunsight the trail turns toward the rocks and ends below the initial third class terrain. By scrambling and walking up and right (north) the area at the base of ROX SALT and UNRELENTING VERTICALITY is soon reached.

It is possible to reach the North Peak - East Face from the South Peak. From Broadway Ledge scramble down and over to the base of the North Peak.

DESCENT

From the end of your route, scramble and walk north along the summit ridge to reach the trail. Either descend along the East Face trail if you want to climb again, or descend via the tourist trail to reach the parking lot.

Many North Peak East face routes are best descended by rappelling, usually from trees.

360 GUNSIGHT TO NORTH PEAK 5.0
This is a long route that can be split into as many pitches as one desires. It starts in the obvious, wide chimney at the northeast corner of the Gunsight Notch. Climb to a ledge which is followed to an inside corner. Ascend the corner to the top of the ridge. Follow the ridge to a chimney then continue to the summit. (400 ft.)
FA   Chuck Sproull, Sally Jordan, Peter Gardiner 1969
The summit ridge is tremendously exposed and has much loose rock.

361 EEYORE'S TAIL 5.3
Start just below the right end of the Gunsight Notch.
#1   Climb up and right on easy ledges to an inside corner. Climb the corner up to an intersection with GUNSIGHT TO NORTH PEAK. This route lies just to the left of the obvious zig-zag flakes which break the lichen covered face. (95 ft.)
FA   John Christian, June Lehman 1971
Protection is adequate with large gear.

GUNSIGHT NOTCH

362 AS YOU LIKEN IT 5.10c R
Start 20 ft. left of LICHEN OR LEAVE IT, at a prominent clean streak with a finger and hand crack. The route lies to the right of EEYORE'S TAIL.
#1 Climb the face to a small overhang. Move through the overhang and up to the tree. (50 ft.)
#2 Climb the face behind the tree for 30 ft. to a small overhang. Traverse right along the roof to the belay tree on LICHEN OR LEAVE IT. (50 ft.)
FA Howard Doyle, Eric Janoscrat, Cal Swoager

Routes #364-368 are located on the wall above LICHEN OR LEAVE IT, ROUX, and FINGER STINGER.

363 A.Y.L.I. DIRECT FINISH 5.10d R
(Var.) At the undercling, move straight up the white streak past 2 bolts.
FA John Govi, Eddie Begoon 1988

364 BEAR'S DELIGHT 5.5 *
This is the prominent right-facing corner at the left end of the ledge above LICHEN OR LEAVE IT and HELTER SKELTER. The bolts and pin of LICHENING BOLT will be on the face to your right.
#1 Climb the corner to its top. Finish on GUNSIGHT TO NORTH PEAK. (40 ft.)
FA John Christian, W. Putnam 1971
If you do this route be prepared for the harrowing traverse of the summit ridge, which is exposed and loose.

365 LICHENING BOLT 5.10b R
(Var.) Climb the face directly above the end of LICHEN OR LEAVE IT. Move past 2 bolts and a poor fixed pin to the tree.
FA Tom Cecil, Steve Cater 1988
Bring TCU's or the like to back up the pin. There is at least a fifteen foot 5.7-5.8 runout at the top.

366 SOME THINGS NEVER CHANGE 5.10a
Find the bolted face behind and right of the tree at the top of the first pitch of ROUX.
#1 Climb straight up the textured face past several quarter-inch bolts (including doubled bolts in one spot). Move right to belay at the crusty old pin anchor above BLUE HIGHWAY, or move on up to the summit ridge.
FA Herb Laeger, Howard Doyle 1991

367 BLUE HIGHWAY 5.9
#1 Climb the face above FINGER STINGER. Climb pockets past a bolt.
FA Mike Artz, Gene Kistler 1985

368 TRAVELER'S REST 5.11b
Begin 15 ft. right of BLUE HIGHWAY.
#1 Climb past 2 bolts then move left to easier ground.
FA Eddie Begoon 1989

Ashton Walton on HELTER SKELTER (5.10c).   (Photo: Darell Hensley)

369 LICHEN OR LEAVE IT 5.8 *
Start at the base of the smooth wall and thin cracks 10 ft. left of the ROUX corner.
#1   Scramble to a large ledge and climb up and left, over moderate but run-out (5.6 R) rock, toward the tree. Climb the obvious right-tending crack to a good tree. (100 ft.)
FA Howard Doyle, Lotus Steele 1976

370 HELTER SKELTER 5.10c *
Use the same start as LICHEN OR LEAVE IT and ROUX. Climb the ROUX corner until about 10 ft. below the tree. Traverse left across the face to a thin crack in the face. Climb the crack to the large tree. (100 ft.)
FA Howard Doyle, Lotus Steele 1976
Take wires including micronuts.

371 KEDS 5.7

Use the same start as ROUX.

#1   Climb ROUX to the traverse that leads to HELTER SKELTER. Move left 3 ft and climb the larger crack up to the ledges. (100 ft.)

FA   John Gathright, Istvan Sugar 1986

372 ROUX 5.2 *

This follows the large left-facing corner to the right of LICHEN OR LEAVE IT.

#1   Climb the corner, mainly using the wall on the right, to a large pine tree on the conspicuous ledge. (90 ft.)

#2   Follow easy rock up and right to the summit. (60 ft.)

FA   Maitland Sharpe, Linda Harris 1971

373 SCREAMLINE 5.10b **X**

Start about 15 ft. left of the very shallow FINGER STINGER corner, beneath a white wall with broken cracks. This route is directly below the rappel tree at the top of the first pitch ROUX.

#1   Climb the face and cracks to the trees above. (45 ft.)

FA   Mel Banks, Greg Hand 1978

Most often toproped. A placement for a hand placed Long Dong is available.

374 INNOCENCE 5.12a **R/X**

Start on SCREAMLINE.

#1   Climb six or eight feet of SCREAMLINE to a bucket/horn, step right to a right slanting hairline crack. Follow this crack to a horizontal crack, then head straight up the unprotected face to join FINGER STINGER at its upper corner.

FA   Ed Begoon (first lead of an existing T.R. problem) 1989

Take a selection of brass and or steel nuts.

375 FINGER STINGER 5.8 **R/X** *

Start beneath a shallow, smooth, left-facing corner which lies only 3 ft. to the left of the bottom of the prominent diagonal crack of UNRELENTING VERTICALITY.

#1   Climb the shallow corner to its top just below the overhang. Move left until the flakes steepen into a narrow left-facing corner. Follow the corner to the large pine. (65 ft.)

#2   Finish on ROUX.

FA   Herb Laeger, Eve Uiga

Unfortunately this excellent line follows an expanding flake (forming the initial narrow corner) and has been the scene of at least three ground falls.

376 UNRELENTING VERTICALITY 5.9 **R** *

Approximately 50 ft. to the right of ROUX there is a prominent crack which diagonals up and right.

#1   Climb the crack, past a steep section, to a small tree on a decent ledge. (65 ft.)

#2   Move right about 15 ft. to a crack which has a tree growing from it. Climb the crack and end with an easy hand traverse to the left. (100 ft.)

FA   Herb Laeger, Eve Uiga, Charlie Rollins 1974

An excellent route, though the crux moves near the ground are difficult to protect.

377 CHALK PARTY 5.9 **R**
Begin about 15 ft. right of UNRELENTING VERTICALITY and just left of ROX SALT.
#1   Climb the thin, left-facing corner to its top. Traverse right across the face to a ledge. Step up and climb a poorly protected face to intersect with the top of UNRELENTING VERTICALITY. (60 ft.)
FA Eric Janoscrat, Mark Shissler 1982

378 ROX SALT 5.7 *
Just right of UNRELENTING VERTICALITY is another right leaning crack.
#1   Climb the crack up and right to an anchor consisting of a bolt and a piton. (50 ft.)
FA Howard Doyle, Lotus Steele 1977

379 REALLY FLAKY 5.7 **R**
Start several feet to the right of ROX SALT just past a small pine growing a few feet up.
#1   Climb a short finger crack to the shallow left-facing corner system. Awkward face moves and stemming lead to the same ledge and anchor as for ROX SALT. Note: If you could be sure the pitons were good this pitch might not rate an R.
#2   Climb straight up to a small tree at an overhanging slab. Move left under the slab then up to finish on ROUX. (60 ft.)
FA Steve Beck, Ed Lacroix 1978

380 SALLY'S PERIL 5.5
Begin a few feet to the right of REALLY FLAKY.
#1 Climb the larger, rougher left-facing corner to a small vegetated ledge. Climb a short left-facing corner to a large ledge with a tree. (80 ft.)
#2 Move up and right to the base of a prominent detached flake. (80 ft.)
#3 Climb the chimney up to the summit. (80 ft.)
FA Chuck Sproull, Sally Jordan, Peter Gardiner 1971

381 GREAT IMPOSTOR 5.9 *
Start between SALLY'S PERIL and PSYCHOPROPHYLAXIS below a crack which diagonals up and right.
#1 Climb the crack up and right past a small bush. Continue up and right, past a run-out section to the ledge and large tree of SALLY'S PERIL. (80 ft.)
#2 Move left across a ramp for 15 ft. to a left-facing corner. Climb the corner and face past an expanding, detached flake to the summit. (45 ft.)
FA Marty McLaughlin, Howard Doyle, Jim Annex 1979
The second pitch is nothing to write home about.

382 WIRE BLISS 5.10d **R**
Start just left of the PSYCHOPROPHYLAXIS corner.
#1 Climb up toward the obvious crack system in the middle of the face. Climb the crack and the slight bulge at its end. Step left and finish on GREAT IMPOSTOR.
FA Howard Doyle, Eric Janoscrat
The pro is shaky but plentiful.

383 PSYCHOPROPHYLAXIS 5.10b *
Start to the right of SALLY'S PERIL beneath an obvious left-facing inside corner.
#1 Climb the corner to its top. Move up and right to the large tree on SALLY'S PERIL. (75 ft.)
#2 From the tree climb the face past an arching left-facing corner straight to the top. (35 ft.)
FA Greg Hand, Hunt Prothro, Herb Laeger 1975
Near the end of the first pitch is an unprotected stretch of moderate rock.

384 SPRINGTIME 5.8
(Var.) From the end of the first pitch of PSYCHOPROPHYLAXIS go straight up the face past a small left facing, arching corner.
FA Howard Doyle, Marty McLaughlin

385 SKIN BRACER 5.9 **R**
Begin about 8 ft. to the right of PSYCHOPROPHYLAXIS, beneath an inside corner.
#1 Climb the corner to the roof. Pass over the roof and into a left-facing corner. Follow the corner to a stance. Step right and climb over a bulge. Move back left and up a blank face to the tree. (80 ft.)
FA Chris Kulczycki, Chris Rowins 1978
There is some loose rock.

386 STATIC KLING 5.11a **R**

Begin about 15 ft. right of PSYCHOPROPHYLAXIS.

#1 Climb cracks and overlaps for 20 ft. Traverse right about 7 ft. to the right-facing corner/flake. Make 2 moves up to clip a bolt. Continue up and slightly left and then back right to a bolt below the broken orange crack/groove. Finish on the crack.

FA Howard Doyle, Eric Janoscrat

Hooks are recommended to protect the territory between the bolts. Remember to place pro at the end of the traverse before moving to the first bolt.

387 THE MEMORIAL 5.10a **X**

Start 15 ft. left of PERMANENT PRESS at an orange and black face.

#1 Move up the black streak and loose black flake. The runout occurs high on the pitch.

FA Pete Absolon

Dedicated to the memory of Buck Harper.

388 PERMANENT PRESS 5.9 **X**

Begin about 12 ft. left of the start of WOLERY.

#1 Climb the wall past the left facing corners and flakes for about 30 ft.. Move left and up toward a scooped out area with orange rock. Step back right to a lichen covered wall, then climb straight to the top. (100 ft.)

FA unknown

389 WOLERY 5.6

Near the center of the North Peak-East Face there is a very prominent arching left-facing corner. Start at a block just left of the corner.

#1 Climb to the top of block. Move up and climb a groove up and left until it is possible to traverse back right to gain the corner. Follow the corner to the top of the flake. (60 ft.)

#2 Step right and climb the corner to the summit. (30 ft.)

FA John Christian, W. Putnam 1971

390 UNLIMITED SKY 5.10c **R**

Begin 3 ft. left of DESPERADO.

#1 Climb through the overhang and continue up the face past a bolt.

FA Don Womack, John Govi 1985

391 DESPERADO 5.9 *

Start approximately 15 ft. right of WOLERY at an inside corner facing left.

#1 Climb the face to the left of the overhang in order to reach the roof. Reach over the overhang then hand traverse right to a left-facing corner. Climb the corner to a ledge. (75 ft.)

#2 Finish on WOLERY.

FA Buddy Guthrie, Dee Dee Guthrie

392 DESPERADO DIRECT 5.11b *

(Var.) Climb straight up the left-facing corner to reach the overhang.

FA John Bercaw, Dennis Udall

393 BANDITO 5.9
Begin 25 ft. right of DESPERADO DIRECT.
#1 Climb the clean diagonal finger crack up and left until it joins the corner above DESPERADO. (50 ft.)
FA Hunt Prothro

394 POWERS OF TEN 5.10a **R**
Use the same start as BANDITO.
#1 Climb BANDITO out to the wide vertical slot. Climb straight up through the wide slot onto the face. Continue up the face to the top. (75 ft.)
FA Paul Anikis, Mark Thesing, Pete Absolon
The protection is difficult. A custom made piece was originally used for the wide slot.

395 BURRITO 5.8
Start halfway between BANDITO and CHRISTOPHER ROBIN.
#1 Climb the short left-facing corner to its top. Move left to flakes. Climb straight up to a ledge. Move left 10 ft. to a broken corner just right of a tree. Climb straight up to a ledge. (80 ft.)
FA Eric Janoscrat, Mike Artz 1984
The flakes are loose and the protection is difficult.

396 NACHO MAN 5.10d
Begin 20 ft. right of BURRITO.
#1 Climb the left-facing flake then move right onto the face.
FA Mike Artz, Eric Janoscrat 1985

397 CHRISTOPHER ROBIN 5.2
Start about 70 ft. to the right of WOLERY.
#1 Scramble up and left over a narrow ledge to a large pine tree. (40 ft.)
#2 Continue left on the ledge then climb a crack to bypass an overhang. Continue to the top. (50 ft.)
FA U.S. Army 1944

398 PROMISCUITY 5.4
(Var.) Follow corners directly to the tree at the end of the first pitch of CHRISTO-PHER ROBIN. (40 ft.)
FA unknown

399 LAZY DAZE 5.7
#1 Climb the face about 6 ft. right of PROMISCUITY. Climb the crack and finish with an off-width. (90 ft.)
FA Rick Fairtrace, Linda Briskey, Bruce McCellan 1983

400 EXPOSITION 5.2
Begin at CHRISTOPHER ROBIN.
#1 Climb the gully up to the base of the rotten inside corner. Climb the corner then step right about 5 ft. to a crack. Climb the crack to the top. (100 ft.)
FA Maitland Sharpe, Linda Harris 1971

401 QUESTION MARK 5.3
#1 At the top of the gully climb up and left toward a notch in the skyline. (95 ft.)
FA Tom Stenger, Rick Varner

402 BLUE EYES 5.7
Use the same start as QUESTION MARK.
#1 Climb a slightly overhanging corner up and right for 35 ft. Continue up and right over small flakes to a ledge beneath the summit. (90 ft.)
FA Bruce Cox, Judi Cox 1983

403 OCTAVE DOCTOR 5.9
Begin just right of and around the corner from EXPOSITION.
#1 Climb shallow, curving, left-facing corners until they end. Step left, around the outside corner. Continue to climb up the face and crack to a ledge. Climb easier rock to a good ledge with fixed pins. (60 ft.)
#2 Climb straight past the pin on flakes and knobs to a ledge. Climb a short crack to the summit. (40 ft.)
FA Sandy Fleming, Johnny Robinson 1982

404 LONG LEGGEDY BEASTIES 5.4
Begin below and left of the prominent "V" notch on the skyline.
#1 Climb the face directly up to the ledge that lies 10 ft. to the left of the "V" notch. (40 ft.)
FA Maitland Sharpe, Linda Harris 1971

405 POOH'S CORNER 5.1
Begin below and just right of the prominent "V" notch.
#1 Climb ledges and an inside corner just to the right of the notch. Walk into the notch. (30 ft.)
FA U.S. Army 1943

406 OH POOH 5.1
Begin right of the "V" notch, beneath a smaller notch.
#1 Climb straight up to the smaller notch. (30 ft.)
FA U.S. Army 1943

407 HEFFALUMP TRAP 5.3
Start about 75 ft. left of the north end of the cliff below a slightly overhanging flake.
#1 Climb up and left along the flake until the top is reached. (40 ft.)
FA U.S. Army 1943

408 HEFFALUMP TRAP DIRECT 5.2
(Var.) Climb the route direct by using the inside corner.
FA U.S. Army 1943

409 HERPES 5.7

Begin about 20 ft. left of STREPTOCOCCUS.

#1 Climb orange colored flakes and shallow left-facing corners to a small ledge. Continue up the short overhanging corner to the left and then up the outside corner to the top. (45 ft.)

FA unknown

410 FALSE LABOR 5.10c **R/X**

This route is squeezed between HERPES and STREPTOCOCCUS.

#1 Climb the face just left of STREPTOCOCCUS.

FA Don Womack, Herb Maher, Mike Gray 1985

411 STREPTOCOCCUS 5.9 *

Start just left of the north end of the cliff.

#1 Climb the face up to a steep right-leaning crack in the orange rock. Follow the crack to its end at a horizontal break. Move up and over the bulge to the top. (50 ft.)

FA Howard Doyle, Lotus Steele 1977

412 SKOSHI GO JU 5.10c **R/X**

Start just right of STREPTOCOCCUS.

#1 Climb the broken face to a small ledge. Climb straight to the top.

FA Don Womack, Mike Cote

Don't use holds on STREPTOCOCCUS or ISADORA'S RUN.

413 ISADORA'S RUN 5.3

Begin about 15 ft. from the north end of the cliff.

#1 Climb the right-facing corner up through the overhang. Continue to the top of the cliff. (25 ft.)

FA Bill Webster, Isadora Duncan Brown 1976

INDEX BY ROUTE

INDEX BY RATING
* -Recommended Routes

5.8

5.10a

5.12a

5.12b

5.12c

5.12d

5.13a